BRAINSTORMS

How to Think
More Creatively
about Communication*

Joseph A. DeVito

Hunter College of the
City University of New York

*or About Anything Else

Brainstorms by Joseph A. DeVito.

ISBN: 0-673-98136-3

96 97 98 99   9 8 7 6 5 4 3 2 1

Welcome to Creative Thinking and to Brainstorms

Brainstorms was written to accompany *Essentials of Human Communication*, Second Edition and *Messages: Building Interpersonal Communication Skills*, Third Edition. In both books *critical* thinking is stressed, with end-of-the-chapter sections in *Essentials* and with marginal notes in *Messages*. This booklet helps complete the thinking emphasis by adding the all important creative thinking component.[1]

Creative and critical thinking work best when they work together. Creative thinking helps you generate ideas, to see different perspectives, to discover new ways of looking at old things. Critical thinking helps you evaluate the validity and usefulness of the ideas.

> Genius, in truth, means little more than the faculty of perceiving in an unhabitual way.
> **—WILLIAM JAMES**

---

[1] These techniques are presented as ways of understanding and mastering the skills of communication in all its dimensions. The techniques themselves, however, may also be related to specific communication concepts (see Table, "Creative Thinking and Related Communication Concepts," at the end of this Welcome section).

A good mind is a lord of a kingdom.

—SENECA

All acts performed in the world begin in the imagination.

—BARBARA GRIZZUTI HARRISON

I submit that creativity is an art—an applied art—a workable art—a teachable art—a learnable art—an art in which all of us can make ourselves more and more proficient, if we will.

—ALEX OSBORN

Understanding the connections between communication and creative thinking will help you get more out of this approach. Communication involves a series of decisions—to speak or remain silent, to respond positively or negatively, to compliment or to criticize, and so on. You can look at each of these decisions as a problem to be solved: "Do I say something now or keep my mouth shut?" "Do I say something positive or do I say what I'm really feeling?" "And if I say what I'm thinking, how will I say it?"

The more options you have at your disposal—for example, the more ways in which you can compliment or criticize—the more likely you will be to select an effective option for your specific and unique communication situation. In this way, you stand a much greater chance of making an effective decision (or solving your problem). Creative thinking gives you a means for generating these options.

Although the emphasis here is on using creative thinking in communication, the techniques and principles of creative thinking apply to all aspects of your personal, social, and professional lives. In fact, throughout this booklet communication applications are mixed in with practical business applications. You may, for example, want to generate ways of solving interpersonal conflicts—in your role as friend, child, parent, lover, or co-worker. Or, you may find the need to generate ideas to boost declining sales or motivate a work team, or design a cover for this book. What type of cover would you design? For all of these situations and many more, the techniques discussed here will help considerably.

Brainstorms explains the nature of creative thinking and presents a variety of techniques helpful in generating ideas and increasing your awareness of and your effectiveness in communication (or in any field). After reading this booklet and working with the exercises, you should be better able to use creative thinking to make more effective communication (and other) decisions and to help solve a variety of communication (and other) problems.

Potential powers of creativity are within us and we have the duty to work assiduously to discover these powers.
—MARTIN LUTHER KING, JR.

Stated more explicitly, after reading this booklet and working with the exercises, you should be able to:

1. define *creative thinking* and explain its values and applications to communication and to business generally

2. describe the characteristics of the creative culture, organization, and person

3. explain the process of creative thinking and how it interacts with critical thinking and communication

4. use the specific creative thinking techniques to generate ideas about communication or about any problem area

Creativity is the soul of the true scholar.
—NNAMDI AZIKIWE

Not every technique, however, will be appropriate to every problem. Some techniques are better suited to some types of problems than others. Because of this, techniques that vary widely in style and potential application are included; in this way, you'll stand a good chance of finding at least one or two for most decisions you have to make or problems you want to solve.

A useful way of mastering these techniques is to read and use each at least once, but preferably two or three times. Bring each technique under conscious control so that you might use any one with equal facility. Then, when you want to solve a problem, you can call up the one or two or three techniques that seem most appropriate.

Do realize that these techniques will not—in themselves—solve a problem. They are merely "tricks" to force your mind to look at your problem in different ways and to generate ideas for dealing with it. To solve a problem, then, seems to involve at least three interrelated processes:

1. Generating ideas (creative thinking)

2. Evaluating ideas (critical thinking)

3. Applying ideas (communication)

These processes interact with each other. Creative and critical thinking share many of the same goals and techniques, and thinking is often both creative and critical at the same time. Sometimes it is neither. Similarly, communication is integrally involved in thinking. In fact, learning theorists John Bransford and Barry Stein (1993) note that

"many experienced writers, speakers, and researchers say that the development of ideas occurs to a great degree during the process of putting ideas into a communicable form." At the risk of oversimplification, we can represent the processes as in the accompanying figure.

Critical Thinking
to evaluate ideas

Creative Thinking
to generate ideas

Communication
to apply ideas

The Creative Thinking, Critical Thinking, Communication Triangle. The process of problem solving can be described as beginning with creative thinking where the ideas are generated, then moving to critical thinking where the ideas are assessed and evaluated, and then to communication where the ideas are presented convincingly and implemented effectively. Yet, there is much interaction, with each process influencing each other process. How effectively does this diagram capture the relationship among these processes? Try creating an alternative visualization.

Creating is the true essence of life.
—REINHOLD NIEBUHR

Some techniques covered in Part Two are presented here for the first time (for example, logographic analysis, add-a-tag groups, and the professionals). Some techniques are developments and expansions of well known theories and principles—the abstraction ladder, for example, derives from the work of the General Semanticists; altercasting from the work of sociologists Weinstein and Deutschberger 1963 (also see McLaughlin 1984); and Galileo and the Ghosts from an idea presented by Roger von Oech's in his insightful *A Whack on the Side of the Head* (1983). Other techniques are presented essentially as they were developed by others; for example, brainstorming and attribute listing are discussed as designed by their originators. In many cases, the same technique is discussed by different writers. Included in the discussion of the techniques are any sources from which I drew ideas or inspiration. These additional sources will prove excellent follow-up reading.

The techniques vary in their level of sophistication and in the detail with which they are presented. Some take little time to work through while others will require a longer time commitment. As already noted, you'll also find that some techniques work well with some problems and prove ineffective with others. You will have to select the techniques to try on the basis of your specific problem and goal.

All techniques in Part Two contain specific exercises integrated into the discussion. Completing these exercises, alone or in groups, will help to further clarify the ideas and techniques and will give you greater control over them. The boxed items present additional thoughts, research findings, and in a few cases, exercises, on creative thinking.

The Sources and Suggested Readings identify the reference sources and offer suggestions for continued reading on creativity. These latter are prefaced by an asterisk (*) and are annotated. Building a personal library in creative thinking will prove useful throughout your personal and professional life, and now is a good time to start.

Connecting Brainstorms To Your Course. Some of these relationships between techniques and communication concepts are quite literal and others are more metaphorical. Connections between the concepts in Brainstorms and additional concepts in *Messages* or *Essentials* should be added as they are found useful. Chapter numbers are suggested in the table below for connecting Brainstorms to specific text chapters in both *Messages*, Third Edition and *Essentials of Human Communication*, Second Edition.

Brainstorms	Related Communication Concepts	*Messages 3/e*	*Essentials 2/e*
Creative Thinking Preliminaries	nature of communication communication skills interpersonal communication group interaction	1, 12	1, 10, 11 cultural viewpoints power perspectives
Creative Visualization	perception self-concept self-esteem	2, 3	2, 3
The Director's Chair	self-concept self-awareness self-esteem self-perception (implicit theories)	2, 3, 7	2, 3
Mindfulness	self-awareness interpersonal effectiveness metaskills perception (first impressions) effective listening	2, 3, 4, 8	2, 3, 4, 7
Sens-ational Thinking	perception nonverbal communication	3, 6	3, 6
Travels in Space and Time	nonverbal communication spatial communication temporal communication static evaluation communication context culture	6, 9	6 cultural viewpoints
Surprise!	empathy other orientation	7, 8	7
The Abstraction Ladder	verbal messages concrete style verbal messages concrete style	5	5, 13
Similarities and Differences	social comparisons definition comparison and contrast	10	8
Exceptional Analysis	cultural maxims beliefs, attitudes, and values	9, 12	15 cultural viewpoints
Attribute Listing and Reversal	definition depth and breadth social penetration speech topics	10	8, 12, 14

Metaphors and Similes	verbal messages style and language ambiguity abstraction	5	5, 13
Checklists	memory perception time management	3, 6	3, 6, 14, 15
Altercasting	conversation social roles and role reversal culture and ethnocentrism credibility	8, 9	7, 15 cultural viewpoints
The Professionals	interviewing problem solving credibility conflict resolution	11	7, 9, 15
Galileo and the Ghosts	interviewing perception research	3	9, 14
Brainstorming	small group communication idea generation group problem solving groups positiveness self-monitoring feedback cooperation and competition	8	10, 11
Focus Groups	information sharing groups group membership group leadership	8	7, 10, 11
Add-a-Tag Groups	small group communication problem solving groups conversation transactional processes group member roles	8	7, 10, 11
Logographic Analysis	perception language emotional communication small group communication	3, 5, 7	3, 5, 10, 11
Postscript: Communicating New Ideas	assertiveness conflict resolution groupthink communication apprehension listening audience analysis	2, 4, 11, 12	2, 4, 7, 10, 11, 12, 13 power perspectives

Acknowledgments

I want to thank the people at HarperCollins, especially acquisition editor Cynthia Biron and developmental editor Dawn Groundwater, who shared my belief that our textbooks should not only teach communication theories and skills but should also teach students how to think about communication—more critically and more creatively. I also want to thank supplements editor Mark Gerrard for seeing this project through from manuscript to finished booklet.

In addition, I am indebted to those reviewers who shared their insights and suggestions with me. Thank you:

Cynthia E. Dewar, City College of San Francisco, California
Joseph Giordano, University of Wisconsin, Eau Claire
Matthew M. Martin, West Virginia University
James Murtha, Harford Community College, Maryland
Patty Richardson, Cecil Community College, Maryland

Contents

Part One

Creative Thinking
Preliminaries

The scientist is a lover of truth for the very love of truth itself, wherever it may lead.
—LUTHER BURBANK

Think about your own creativity. How creative are you? In thinking about your answer, did you focus on your major creative efforts (the painting you created, the poem you wrote, the corporate merger you put together, or the invention you developed)? These are your **peak creativity** accomplishments and are the type of creative efforts many think of when they hear the word creative. But, there is another type of creativity, your **extent of involvement.** This type of creativity manifests itself in the ways in which you tackle everyday issues, for example, the dinners you prepare, the letters you write, the advice you give others (Richards, Kinney, Benet, and Merzel 1988). This booklet is designed to increase the likelihood and frequency of peak creative episodes and to increase your creativity in your everyday efforts to deal with the world.

> If you have one good idea, people will lend you twenty.
>
> —MARIE VON EBNER-ESCHENBACH

Because understanding the nature of creative thinking will help you prepare for your own creative thinking experiences, let's begin by discussing:

- what creative thinking is
- the values you can derive from creative thinking
- the characteristics of the creative culture, organization, and person
- the critical thinking process (the stages you would normally go through in creating ideas)

What Is Creative Thinking?

Here are a few definitions to get you started on what creative thinking is and how you can be more creative in your own thinking. Notice that the emphasis in these definitions—as in the growing literature on creative thinking—is on **newness** and **value** or **usefulness**. Newness alone—according to most theorists—is not sufficient to qualify as creative.

Creativity is the ability to look at the same thing as everyone else but to see something different.
—CHARLES THOMPSON

> Creative thinking is the ability "to produce new ideas and fresh insights which are of value to that individual" (Olson 1980).

> "Creativity is the skill to originate the new and to make the new valuable" (Higgins 1994).

> ". . . [the] capacity to produce new ideas, insights, inventions or artistic objects, which are accepted as being of social, spiritual, aesthetic, scientific or technological value" (Vernon 1986).

> "The creative individual is a person who regularly solves problems, fashions products, or defines new questions in a domain in a way that is initially considered novel but that ultimately becomes accepted in a particular cultural setting" (Gardner 1993).

At its most basic level, creativity is the process of combining two or more ideas into a new and useful idea. The techniques of creative thinking are nothing more (but nothing less either) than stimuli to help you combine two ideas in ways that will produce a new and useful third idea.

• **Try exploring creativity** by having each member of the group or class select the three people he or she feels are the most creative. Each member should briefly tell the group why he or she selected these persons. Here are a few names to get you started thinking about creative individuals in a wide variety of fields (but do add your own): Maya Angelou, Isaac Newton, Enrico Fermi, Alexander the Great, Oprah Winfrey, Agatha Christie, Mother Teresa, Muhammad, Jesus, Confucius, Napoleon, Gandhi, Cleopatra, Dalai Lama, Genghis Khan, John Grisham, Einstein, Galileo, Madonna, Michael Jackson, Michaelangelo, Elvis Presley, Henry Ford, Grandma Moses, Sting, Bill Clinton, Hillary Clinton, Martin Luther King Jr., Horatio Alger, John Lennon, Walt Disney, Karl Marx, Thomas Jefferson, Chaucer, Julia Child, Thomas Aquinas, Victor Hugo, Betty Friedan, Rembrandt, Chopin, Leonardo DaVinci, Bill Gates, Steven Spielberg, Robert DeNiro, Jodie Foster.

Creativity: "the ability to introduce order into the randomness of nature."

—ERIC HOFFER

Originality is simply a fresh pair of eyes.

—WOODROW WILSON

Another way to explore the meanings of creativity (especially as applied to the workplace) is to have each group member read over the following list of occupations (or add your own) and identify how creativity might help each of these professionals: fine artists, photographers, accountants, reporters, editors, scientists, psychologists, actors, farmers, novelists, poets, small business owners, management, sales people, talk show hosts, used car dealers, college teachers, college administrators, police officers.

Five Styles of Thinking

Allen F. Harrison and Robert M. Bramson (1984) identify five main types of thinking.

- The **synthesist** combines a variety of different things into something new; wants to integrate diverse elements into a new meaningful whole.

- The **idealist** looks for ideal solutions to problems and is greatly concerned with the impact of different solutions on people. The idealist asks, what is good for the world?

- The **pragmatist** is practical and looks for solutions that will get the job done. The important question is "What will work?"

- The **analyst** looks for the one best solution that almost invariably is the scientific solution. The analyst asks, "What's the most logical solution?"

- The **realist** looks for concrete results and is concerned with identifying the relevant facts in any given decision process.

Which type(s) are you? Does your particular thinking style prevent you from exploring or thinking about other perspectives? Because creativity depends on mixing the various thinking styles, consider how you might incorporate the other styles into your general thinking pattern.

Two dimensions of creativity will help to further define this important concept. These dimensions are **fluency** and **flexibility** (Guilford 1975).

There are no evil thoughts except one: the refusal to think.

—AYN RAND

Fluency

Fluency refers to the number of concepts you can generate in a fixed amount of time. Thus, the more uses for a specific item or the more potential solutions to problems that you can generate, the greater your fluency.

> A thought is often original, though you have uttered it a hundred times.
>
> —**OLIVER WENDELL HOLMES, SR.**

• **Try experimenting with fluency** by having all members of a group or class list the uses for a common object (an empty mustard jar, an 8" x 8" x 2" piece of wood, a teapot, a toothbrush—a test originally developed by J. P. Guilford) on anonymously written index cards. Or the group might address more relationship oriented problems; for example, what can we do to improve interpersonal communication at home or on the job? After about three minutes, the cards are collected and read to the entire group. The more uses listed on the card, the more fluent the individual. This exercise should also illustrate that the group is a lot more fluent than any individual, a useful realization when participating in small groups. Try some variation of the fluency exercise either alone or with a group.

This exercise will also give you a good idea of how fluent you are in relation to others in your group. Following the techniques and principles of creative thinking presented here should increase your fluency.

Flexibility

Flexibility refers to your ability to switch gears and think in different directions. Think back to the fluency exercise where members identified the uses for a common object. Some members probably thought of uses from a wide variety of fields, whereas others focused on one or two narrow fields. For example, in the uses of a toothbrush, if you gave all cleaning uses you would be showing less flexibility than if you gave cleaning uses plus uses in gardening, decorating, and cooking, for example. A good example of flexibility is very likely the thinking that went into identifying the wide uses of a product such as baking soda—it's used in cleaning clothes, cooking, deodorizing, brushing teeth. Another example is the widely different foods that can be prepared with a product such as Bisquick. The flexibility with which you can use these products is largely responsible for their enormous success.

> Any activity becomes creative when the doer cares about doing it right, or better.
> **—JOHN UPDIKE**

• **Try your hand at flexibility** by generating ways of having a good time on Saturday night or uses for an 8"(L) x 8"(W) x 4"(H)" wooden box. One procedure is to have independently operating small groups generate as many possible answers to the question. After a set amount of time, the answers of each group are read aloud. Classify the solutions into major categories. The number of different distinct categories identified would be a measure of flexibility.

Some Assumptions about Creativity

A number of assumptions underlie this presentation of creative thinking and these need to be identified here. Perhaps most important is the assumption that **creativity can be learned**; it can be increased. Regardless of the level of creativity on which you are now functioning, you can progress to a higher level. Put differently, we are all creative to some degree and that degree can be increased.

> We all have ability. The difference is how we use it.
> —**STEVIE WONDER**

Creativity is always relevant. Regardless of what you are working on, creativity can be of assistance. Creativity is relevant to your interpersonal relationships and will prove of value in solving problems, improving your relationship life, and resolving interpersonal conflicts. Creativity will also prove of great value in your professional life. Regardless of what profession you are in, you will have problems to solve and situations to make better and creative thinking will help greatly. On another level, creativity will prove of value to you in all communication situations: conversations with friends, lovers, and family; interviewing, small groups and work teams, and in public and mediated communication.

> There is no subject so old that something new cannot be said about it.
> —**FYODOR DOSTOEVSKY**

Opportunities for creativity exist everywhere. Something does not have to be broken to be fixed. Most things that aren't broken can be improved or made better; hence, the ubiquitous value of creative thinking.

Creativity is universal across all areas of knowledge and experience. This booklet focuses on communication, probably the most important of all your behaviors. But creative thinking will prove of value in any discipline (the arts and humanities, the social sciences, and the sciences).

Individual ideas—like breaths—are waiting to be drawn from unlimited supply.
—MARGARET DANNER

Creativity will never not be needed. There will always be a need for creativity. Unlike the head of the patent office who said in 1899: "everything that can be invented has been invented" (and wanted to close the patent office), we assume that inventions and discoveries will continue as long as humans exist.

Patents as a Measure of Creative Thinking

In the United States patents are issued to an individual who has discovered or invented something new and useful. The patent prohibits others from developing or using the newly invented device or design for a seventeen year period. If patents are taken as an index of creativity, then creativity is increasing. In 1980, for example, approximately 66,000 patents were issued, in 1990, 99,100 were issued. Of these, some 52,000 were issued to United States citizens and some 47,000 to residents of other countries. Japan leads with almost 21,000, Germany is second with almost 7,900, and France is third with almost 3,100. Rounding out the top ten are the United Kingdom, Canada, Italy, Switzerland, Netherlands, Sweden, and Taiwan.

The number of patents also varies greatly from one state to another. Californians are issued the largest number of patents: over 7,900 in 1990. New York was second with over 4,500 and Texas was third with almost 3,200. New Jersey, Illinois, Pennsylvania, Ohio, Minnesota, Massachusetts, and Florida followed.

The Values of Creative Thinking

Creativity is needed in all times. But, perhaps because of other developments, creativity seems especially useful today. For example, the rapidly changing technologies create new problems at a faster rate than the slower developments our parents and grandparents had to contend with. Creative solutions must be found for a wide variety of economic, scientific, social, and interpersonal problems.

> We do not live to think, but, on the contrary, we think in order that we may succeed in surviving.
> —ORTEGA Y CASSET

Today, we live in a global marketplace. Without creative developments we lose the ability to compete, whether in farming, manufacturing, distribution, or in the actual development of new and useful products and services.

Creative thinking is also strongly related to professional effectiveness. Your advancement in a corporation (and probably your morale), for example, is likely to depend in part on your creative abilities and how you deal with the creativity of others. Creative thinking increases your ability to contribute ideas and perspectives on work teams and task groups and

> Creativity not committed to public purpose is merely therapy or ego satisfaction.
> —ERNEST A. JONES

should thus help you become a more effective and more valued team member.

And, of course, the ability to generate ideas and solve problems will invariably increase personal power. In a similar way, creative thinking is likely to make you a more interested and a more interesting individual. Rather than being a reactor to the ideas of others, creative thinking enables you to participate in and control your own environment. You will be better able to develop the ideas you need to accomplish your purposes and goals.

Creative thinking makes everyday life a little easier by solving many of the small problems we have to deal with on a day to day basis such as entertaining the children on a rainy Saturday afternoon or partitioning your hard drive.

Creative thinking also gives you a sense of accomplishment and is likely to increase your self-esteem. After all, one way we judge ourselves is through our ability to generate ideas, our ability to solve problems.

Creative thinking enables you to see different perspectives on an issue and thus increases the likelihood of your perceptual accuracy. When you can see more, you're more likely to get a more complete and more accurate picture. And this holds true whether you're perceiving a person, an event, or a belief. Perhaps the most general value is that creative thinking helps you to maximize your potential as a sensing, thinking, communicating individual.

Creative thinking helps you solve problems and improve your way of doing just about everything, from resolving an interpersonal conflict to advancing through the corporate hierarchy. The Creativity in Communication Pyramid is designed to give you some idea of the areas of communication to which creative thinking is applicable (Figure 1).

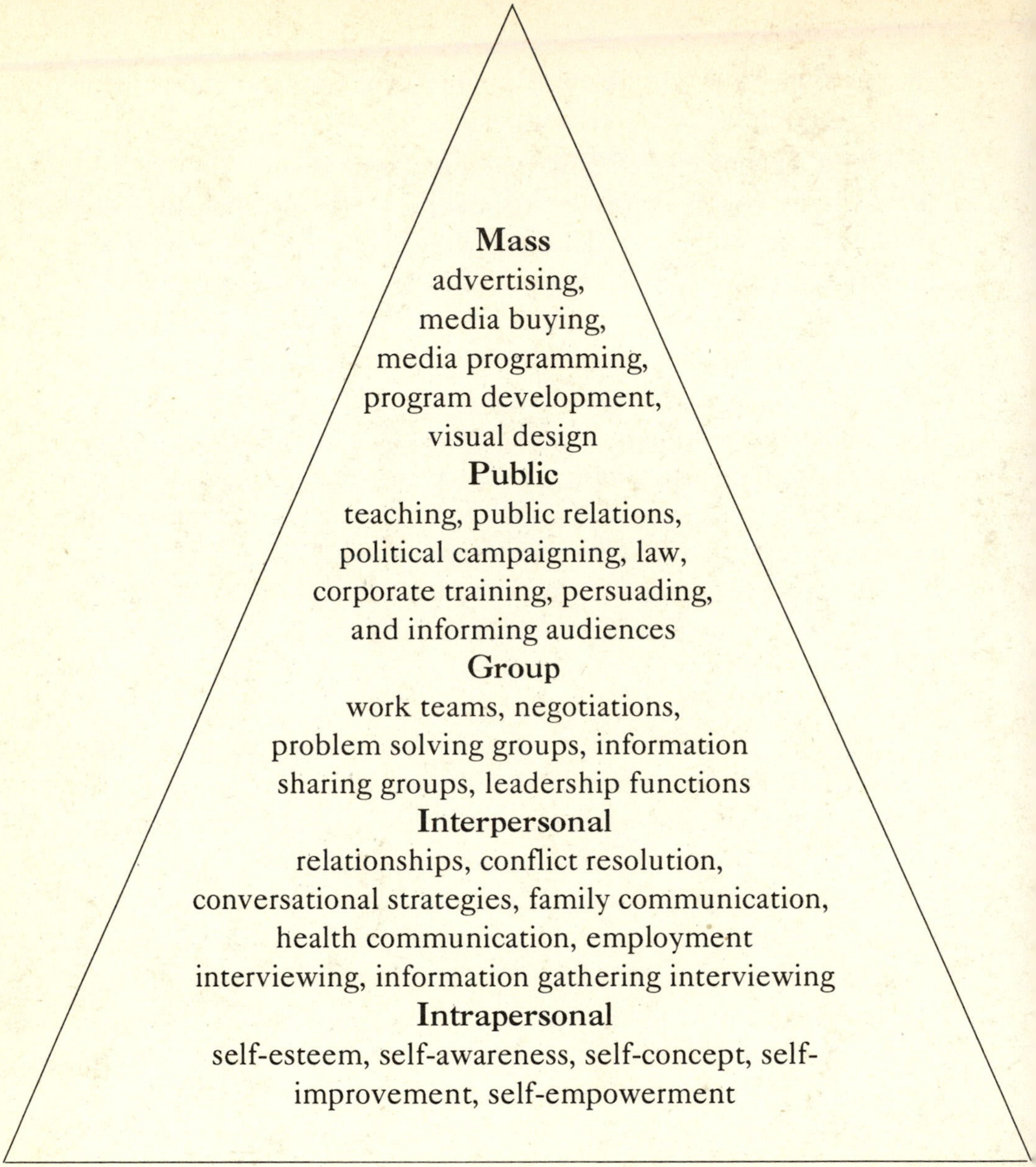

Mass
advertising,
media buying,
media programming,
program development,
visual design
Public
teaching, public relations,
political campaigning, law,
corporate training, persuading,
and informing audiences
Group
work teams, negotiations,
problem solving groups, information
sharing groups, leadership functions
Interpersonal
relationships, conflict resolution,
conversational strategies, family communication,
health communication, employment
interviewing, information gathering interviewing
Intrapersonal
self-esteem, self-awareness, self-concept, self-
improvement, self-empowerment

Figure 1. The Creativity in Communication Pyramid.

The needs and opportunities for creativity occur across the entire spectrum of communication experiences. Try identifying specific situations in any of these areas where creative thinking would prove of value.

• **Try exploring creativity** by asking members of a small group or entire class to write down at least five questions about communication. The questions don't have to be of any theoretical or practical importance; the only requirement is that they are questions. After everyone has written their questions, the papers should be collected and read to the entire group. By trying this, it should be clear that there are many perspectives that can be brought to bear on a subject, and that your own perspective is just one of the many possibilities.

> A new idea is a light that illuminates presences which simply had no form for us before the light fell on them.
> **—SUSANNNE K. LANGER**

The Creative Culture, Organization, and Person

Do cultures differ in creativity? Do some cultures encourage while others discourage creativity? Why are some organizations more creative than others? What enables some organizations to consistently develop new products and successfully revise old ones? How does the creative person differ from the uncreative person? What makes one person inventive and another uninventive?

> Progress might have been all right once, but it's gone on too long.
> **—OGDEN NASH**

Culture and Creativity

Certain characteristics of culture seem to encourage while other characteristics seem to discourage creativity. Here are some characteristics that have been identified as encouraging creativity (Fabun, n.d.).

First, the creative culture **has sufficient material wealth** so that its members are free of the concerns for subsistence—concerns that leave little time for creative exploration. If members are focused on securing food, for example, they will have little time or energy for thinking about much else. In a similar way, if you are going to college full time and are not working and have no family obligations, you would be able to devote a lot more time to "just thinking" than would the more typical college student who also works and has a variety of family obligations.

Second, the creative culture maintains an **efficient, open, and free communication system** so that members may share ideas with few restrictions. In the very near future, electronic communication and, for example, the Internet, will provide members of all cultures with this free and open access to information.

Third, the creative culture **rewards rather than punishes creativity**. Its educational system must also reward creativity and encourage free inquiry rather than being solely concerned with passing on what is already known. Prizes for creative efforts,

> I gnorance, arrogance, and racism have bloomed as Superior Knowledge in all too many universities.
>
> **—ALICE WALKER**

> M ost higher education is devoted to affirming the traditions and origin of an existing elite and transmitting them to new members.
>
> **—MARY CATHERINE BATESON**

> C reative minds always have been known to survive any kind of bad training.
>
> **—ANNA FREUD**

from the Nobel to that of the local high school, are examples of such rewards.

Fourth, the creative culture provides its members with **opportunities for privacy**. The culture must allow its members sanctuaries for relatively long term and uninterrupted research. A tenured professorship at a research institution is a good example of one such opportunity.

Finally, the creative culture gives its members the **ability to form peer groups**. It allows and encourages the formation and maintenance of professional associations. Professional academic associations—to which many of your instructors belong—and computer discussion groups are good examples of peer groups built around mutual interest in a field of study.

Organizations and Creativity

Like the general culture, the organization (political, religious, business, educational) can also foster or hinder the development of creative thinking. Hanley Norins (1990)— one of the leaders in creative thinking at Young and Rubicam advertising agency— suggests five characteristics of the creative organization.

> No brain is stronger than its weakest think.
> —**THOMAS L. MASSON**

1. **Sets high goals:** the creative organization commits its members and the organization as a whole to high standards.

2. **Develops and maintains an organizational culture:** the creative organization has a company culture—a set of be-

liefs, attitudes, and approaches to problem solving that are consistent over time and that are communicated to all members of the organization.

3. **Rewards creativity:** the creative organization provides rewards and incentives—financial rewards such as bonuses and social rewards such as praise and public recognition—for creative contributions.

4. **Strives for frequent renewal:** the creative organization welcomes change and involves its members in such changes and keeps events stimulating.

5. **Provides the best tools and training:** the creative organization makes the best tools (for example, offices, computer facilities) and the best training (for example, tutors, guest speakers, workshops, open communication) available to all members of the organization.

Creations, whether they are children, poems, or oganizations, take on a life of their own.

—STARHAWK

Personality and Creativity

Research on personality and creativity has identified several personality characteristics that are especially important to creativity (Wade and Tavris 1993).

Creative thinkers are **nonconformists.** Creative thinkers are will-

The creative person is both more primitive and more cultivated, more destructive, a lot madder and a lot saner, than the average person.

—FRANK BARRON

ing to take risks, to appear foolish, for example, in front of colleagues. They are less concerned with what others think of them. Thus, they are more likely to pursue their ideas rather than simply file them away.

Creative thinkers are **independent**. They prefer to work alone (generally) but are not necessarily anti-social.

Creative thinkers are **confident** in their abilities and do not fear failure; they welcome the uncertainty that accompanies creative efforts. They realize, perhaps unconsciously, that it is only through failure that you can learn and that failure, in many ways, brings you one step closer to the solution.

> Living in a state of psychic unrest, in a Borderland, is what makes poets write and artists create.
>
> —GLORIA ANZALDUA

Creative thinkers are **curious** about many things, rather than being narrowly focused on one area. Although they immerse themselves in their own subject, they also want to know about areas outside this subject area. As a result, creative thinkers are often able to see comparisons and contrasts with other areas that help them generate ideas.

Creative thinkers, once they get the idea, are **persistent** in developing and applying it. They are not content to think of the idea and then forget it; they want to develop the idea, explain it to others, and put it into operation.

Table 1 summarizes the three sets of creativity characteristics. Notice that some of the same characteristics are repeated in two columns (for example, the importance of rewards in the culture and in the organization). Notice too that some characteristics are not entirely consistent and may even conflict with each other (for example, the independence in the person with the opportunity to form peer groups in the culture). What characteristics would you include under the heading "the creative family"?

Table 1.
Creativity characteristics in the culture, organization, and person.

The Creative Culture	The Creative Organization	The Creative Person
Possesses sufficient material wealth	Sets high goals	Nonconformist
Fosters open communication	Develops organizational culture	Independent
Rewards creativity	Rewards creativity	Confident
Provides for privacy	Strives for frequent renewal	Curious
Encourages the formation of peer groups	Makes the best tools and training available	Persistent

The Creative Thinking Process

A common general model of problem solving consists of a series of steps or stages such as the following:

- Define and analyze the problem
- Establish criteria for evaluating solutions
- Identify possible solutions
- Evaluate solutions according to the criteria established in Step 2
- Select the best solution(s)
- Implement solution(s)

The creative thinking process involves a similar but not identical series of steps. These steps will further define creative thinking and will give you a clearer idea of the general critical thinking process.

Divergent and Convergent Thinking

Cognitive theorists make the distinction between divergent and convergent thinking that will shed additional light on the creative thinking process. In **divergent thinking**, you begin with a problem and try to generate as many possible solutions as you can. You rarely stick to one set pattern of problem solving or one way of looking at your problem. Rather, you seek different perspectives and a variety of solutions. The techniques for encouraging creativity thinking in Part Two are largely devices to stimulate divergent thinking. Some divergent thinkers may have trouble being practical and critical when it comes time for evaluation of the ideas or their implementation. In **convergent thinking**, you begin with a variety of ideas and try to combine them into one workable solution. For example, out of all the suggestions made by employees to increase morale, you try to pull them together into a meaningful and responsive solution. You might, for example, following a prescribed problem solving sequence to help you arrive at your final solution. In contrast to divergent thinkers, some convergent thinkers may have trouble developing new perspectives.

Although not identical, divergent thinking is more akin to creative thinking (making use of ideas that are new and unexplored) and convergent thinking is more akin to critical thinking (making use of logical reasoning). As you can see, both are necessary for maximum effectiveness.

Phase 1. Recognize the Problem

Creative thinking usually begins with the recognition that something needs to be done. It doesn't have to be a big problem or even one of any great significance, just one that can be corrected or improved. It can be an interpersonal problem ("I don't seem to have many friends") or one in business ("How can we sell more widgets"). Obviously the more important the problem, the more motivation there will be to solve it.

Phase 2. Collect Information

As with any kind of thinking, the more information you have, the more thoroughly you will be able to pursue your subject. Saturate yourself with as much information as you can. Information will enable you to see more than you would see with less information. This step is often omitted by those who assume that a creative idea occurs spontaneously and in a vacuum. Creative ideas are actually more likely to occur to those who have a great deal of information about the topic. The reason is simple: ideas are the result of a new arrangement of, or perspective on, what you have in your brain. The more information you have, the greater the likelihood of new and useful combinations being formed. This is the reason most innovations in a particular field are made by experts in those fields. The plumber is the one most likely to produce innovative ideas on plumbing and the educator is the one most likely to produce innovations in teaching. Rarely do we find plumbers making educational innovations or teachers designing new plumbing devices.

Thinking for Ideas

Prolific writer Isaac Asimov (1983), author of hundreds of books and articles, once said: "The most common and the most effective method for getting an idea is to sit down and think as hard as you can. . . . When Newton was asked where he managed to get his remarkable insights, he said, 'By thinking and thinking and thinking about it'." "When people ask me," continues Asimov, "where I get my ideas, I always say 'By thinking very hard,' and they are clearly disillusioned. Anyone, they seem to decide, can do **that**. Well, if anyone can, then **you** do it, and don't be ashamed of it, either."

Phase 3. Allow Time for Incubation

Incubation is the period during which your unconscious works on the information. It is the period of relaxation during which ideas and creative solutions may be generated. During incubation your problem and possible solutions are allowed to gel, to interact, to grow. You can see incubation in the common situation where you work on a problem for perhaps days and only after you are away from it for a time—sometimes hours, sometimes days—the solution (better than any you had originally thought of) occurs to you. Oddly enough, this idea may occur even when you might be engaged in some totally

Freedom from the desire for an answer is essential to the understanding of a problem.
—**J. KRISHNAMURTI**

unrelated activity. "All the really good ideas I ever had," noted famed American artist Grant Wood, "came to me while I was milking a cow."

Incubation seems to work because it forces you to get away from the problem and thereby allows you to overcome your tendency to look at the problem in one and only one way. When you work on other problems—dealing with other types of information—you allow yourself the opportunity to form associations between information from the original problem and from this new problem.

Sit in reverie, and watch the changing color of the waves that break upon the idle seashore of the mind.

—LONGFELLOW

Problem solving meetings that must reach a solution immediately may not leave time for incubation. Sometimes it may be helpful for a business group to meet, say, from 10-12, break for lunch to allow for incubation, and then reconvene at 2 p.m.. Or perhaps instead of a four-hour meeting on Monday, have a two-hour meeting on Monday and another two-hour meeting on Thursday or Friday. Papers, projects, and even studying for tests should be started early to allow time for incubation and for the creative ideas to emerge.

Not Thinking for Ideas

Creative ideas, according to some researchers, are forever coming into your brain (Stine and Benares, 1994). In fact, you can hardly stop ideas from developing. But, often—perhaps because of your preoccupation with other matters—they don't get a chance to develop fully enough. To allow time for this needed development, one brain researcher (Rossi 1989) suggests that you periodically stop whatever you are doing and just take a

---

> break—relax and try to think of nothing for 20 minutes. During this time, you are likely to experience a flood of creative ideas.

Phase 4. Think about Solutions

At this stage you think about potential solutions, usually with some pretty hard conscious thinking (as described in the box; "Thinking for Ideas"). Sometimes, of course, solutions to your problem suggest themselves while you're thinking of something totally different (as in the box, "Not Thinking for Ideas"). When this happens, count yourself especially fortunate. Sometimes solutions emerge from just casually thinking about the problem without any formal plan or without using any specific technique. Most often, solutions emerge with the help of some hard thinking, often aided by using one or more of the techniques discussed later in this booklet. During this phase, try to think of as many solutions as possible. Try not to censor yourself or resist developing ideas because of a negative first judgment. Also, try not to select a solution before you've had a chance to entertain other possibilities.

> Knowledge rests not upon truth alone, but upon error also.
> —CARL G. JUNG

Phase 5. Evaluate the Solutions

After the solutions have emerged and you've "listened" to them fairly, you can effectively enter the critical thinking stage and begin to evaluate them. Typically, you'll just need one possible solution so be prepared to reject more than you accept. Not all solutions have to be great; just one of them needs to be workable and to represent an improvement. Critical thinking tools such as Edward deBono's six hats technique, discussed in your text, will prove particularly helpful at this stage.

Phase 6. Apply the Best Solution

Essayist William Hazlitt once observed, "Great thoughts reduced to practice become great acts." Your last step, then, involves your communication skills and involves applying the solution you think is best. Your textbook covers these skills in detail and a Postscript in this booklet applies these skills to communicating about new ideas. At first you might try the solution only in your mind and then put it into actual practice. Most solutions can be changed. So, apply them tentatively. Allow for the possibility that you might change them as conditions change or as you gain new information and new perspectives on the problem.

I do not pretend to know what many ignorant men are sure of.
—**CLARENCE DARROW**

The techniques in Part Two are valuable for helping you to creatively explore the nature of the problem (Phase 1), to collect information, from people, nature, science, and the arts (Phase 2), and especially to think about solutions (Phase 4). Allow your unconscious to dominate Phase 3 (incubation), your critical thinking to dominate Phase 5 (evaluation), and communication to dominate Phase 6 (application and implementation).

Creativity, IQ, and Failure

Two factors that many people assume go together with creativity are intelligence and success (Stine and Benares 1994). However, there may be less truth in this assumption than you might at first think. It does seem that a minimum level of intelligence is needed for creativity. Thus, two people with IQ scores of say 85 and 100 are likely to be equally uncreative; and two people with IQ scores of, say, 120 and 150 are likely to be equally creative (Peters 1990). The likely reason for this is that the verbal and logical skills that are needed for creativity also figure prominently in IQ. Thus, the person who has the verbal and logical skills needed for creativity would also score above average in IQ. However, increased intelligence (say above 115 which is about the average for college students), does not seem to result in any increase in creativity.

Further, it seems that failure, not success, may be more closely related to creativity. People we would regard as creative produce lots of ideas and consequently have lots of failures. What seems to make creative people different is that they keep trying. They realize that not every idea can be a winner, and that periodic failures are part of the normal creativity process.

Self-Assessment 1:
How Creative Do You See Yourself?

Before turning to Part Two in which specific techniques of creative thinking are presented, consider your own creativity by responding to the following questions. At the end of this booklet, these questions are addressed again. You may find it interesting to compare your responses.

1. On the basis of your past performance, how creative do you see yourself?

   _____ very creative
   _____ fairly creative
   _____ in the middle
   _____ fairly uncreative
   _____ very uncreative

2. How often do you get creative ideas?

   _____ at least once a day
   _____ a few a week
   _____ a few a month
   _____ one a month
   _____ less than one a month

3. In what areas are you most creative? For example, in what academic areas are you most creative? Least creative? Can you identify any possible reasons for the differences?

4. In what aspects of your personal, social, and professional life does creativity now play a role?

5. What role will creative thinking have in your life 10 years from now?

6. Have you ever had what you would consider a peak creative experience? Describe it.

7. What was your last creative idea? What did you do with it? [This is a tough question but a very revealing one, so take your time to write as detailed a description as you can.]

Part Two

Creative Thinking Techniques

I do not approve of
anything which tampers
with natural ignorance.
—OSCAR WILDE

A variety of creative thinking techniques, along with extensions and combinations, are presented in this section. Before introducing these techniques, consider a few general guidelines for becoming a more creative individual.

I f you think education is expensive, try ignorance.

—DEREK BOK

Acquiring Information

Read a variety of different types of material, for example, plays, newspapers, novels, how to books, poetry, and even comic books and children's books. Also, try to expose yourself to different points of view; avoid falling into the trap of reading only that which supports your current positions. The more diverse your reading—in type and point of view—the more likely you will be able to see issues and problems from different perspectives. Similarly, expose yourself to the best that television has to offer—especially programs that can provide you with new and different perspectives.

Interact with different people and participate in different experiences—especially people and experiences of different cultures. Seeing an issue from the viewpoint of someone of the opposite sex, or of a different affectional orientation, or of a very different age, religion, or culture can give you insights you might not have considered before. Pride yourself on your diversity of thought rather than on single mindedness. Similarly, try to interact with idea-people as much as possible; the more creative your associates, the more creativity is likely to become an important part of your life.

Thinking about Your Decision or Problem

Avoid thinking through filters of unstated assumptions. For example, ask yourself how your political or religious beliefs might be influencing your view of a problem. If you are a conservative Republican, ask how a liberal Democrat or Socialist would see the problem. If you are deeply religious, ask yourself how an atheist would view the problem. Do you have gender biases that lead you to see the behavior of one sex more positively than the very same behavior in the other sex? If so, try to see the problem from the perspective of the opposite sex.

Massage your problem. Creative thinking is often helped by your focusing on the problem itself, rephrasing it, writing it, saying it in different ways or in different languages. Twist it and turn it in any way you'd like. Your objective is to gain a different perspective on the problem, so massage it in any way you can.

> I have no riches but my thoughts,
> Yet these are wealth enough for me.
> —**SARA TEASDALE**

Introduce physical and psychological change. If, for example, you find yourself at an impasse sitting at your desk, get up and take a walk. Or change the popular music on your radio to rap or opera. Or turn on the television and get involved in a soap opera for 10 or 15 minutes. Then return to your desk. You may find yourself looking at your problem from a totally different perspective.

Approaching Creative Thinking Techniques

In approaching these creative thinking techniques:

1. Personalize the techniques. Try to see how these techniques might be useful to your own situation, your own problems. Also, after you use a technique as described here a few times, you may want to alter the technique and modify it so that it is more suited to your purposes. After all, the objective is to develop techniques that are useful to you.

2. Look at how these techniques can work, rather than look for problems in the techniques themselves. The techniques are only useful if you use them. Be open minded about creativity and about the usefulness of the techniques.

3. Try to combine the techniques as seems reasonable. For example, during creative visualization (where you visualize your problem solved), it is wise to also apply the brainstorming rule of "no criticism allowed."

4. In many instances, it may be helpful to attack your problem in small pieces rather than as a whole. The techniques may not fit the problem as a whole but might prove effective on each of the smaller pieces. For example, you may find that a broad problem ("How can this company regain its leadership?") fails to yield to your creative thinking techniques. But, individual parts of this question—"How can we attract the best young minds?" "How can we improve our training program?" "How can we increase worker morale?"—may be addressed quite effectively by a variety of creative thinking techniques.

Respecting Your Ideas

Pocket pen and pad. The obvious reason to carry a pen and pad with you (or a tape recorder or pocket computer), of course, is to record any thoughts you might have that you don't want to risk forgetting. If you've ever failed to remember an idea or bit of information because you didn't write it down, you'll appreciate the value of the ready pad and pen. By writing down ideas, you'll also stand a better chance of going back to these ideas and developing and cultivating them. These alone are reasons enough to carry the pen and pad. But, another, less obvious but more important, reason is that in carrying the pen and pad, you are telling yourself that you will have ideas that are worth remembering and recording. This act of creative self-affirmation is your first step to a more creative day.

Create an idea bank/file —in a notebook, on index cards, or in some computer file. Treat your ideas with respect; as Henry David Thoreau put it: "Associate reverently, as much as you can, with your loftiest thoughts." Your thoughts and ideas are your most valuable assets. Treat them as works in progress; they don't have to be earth-shattering, they need only be different ways of seeing things. File them, organize and reorganize them, play with them. If people gave as much attention to their ideas as they do to their hair, the world would be swimming in ideas.

> The world is before you, and you need not take it or leave it as it was when you came in.
> —JAMES BALDWIN

> Never perish a good thought.
> —MALCOLM FORBES

Thinking Like a Creative Thinker

Think and act like a creative thinker. In thinking about creative thinking, be careful that you do not polarize and see, for ex-

> **N**ever try to discourage thinking, for you are sure to succeed.
> **—BERTRAND RUSSELL**

ample, popular geniuses and artists as creative, and the rest of the world (perhaps including yourself) as uncreative. We are all creative to some extent. Similarly, beware of labeling yourself with the verb "to be"—where you say, for example, "I *am* uncreative." If you define yourself in this way, you'll understandably have difficulty in acting creatively. The most important distinction between those who think creatively and those who don't is not intelligence or education. The major distinction is that creative thinkers act like creative thinkers. They believe they can think creatively and they allow themselves the opportunity to think creativity.

> **W**hether you believe you can do a thing or not, you are right.
> **—HENRY FORD**

Engage in creative affirmation. The practice of affirming oneself as a worthy and capable individual is a standard device used to increase self-esteem and self-empowerment. The technique involves repeating supportive messages to yourself and reflecting on your strengths and virtues. It can also be used to highlight and develop particular abilities. Here is a beginning list of affirmations for asserting to yourself your own creative potential. As you read and reflect on the techniques in this book, more ideas for affirmations will occur to you. Add them to this list. Personalize the list to reflect your own personality, abilities, and goals.

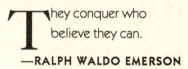

> **T**hey conquer who believe they can.
> **—RALPH WALDO EMERSON**

• **Try affirming yourself** by reflecting on each of these affirmations.

I can see different sides to an issue.

I'm open minded to new experiences.

I'm creative.

I can usually develop appropriate strategies to get what I want.

I'm a pretty active thinker.

I'm interesting to others.

I rarely get locked into one perspective.

I can work well under pressure.

I will not be afraid to fail.

I will allow myself to create, to think of wild ideas.

I will ask questions of even commonly accepted ways of doing things.

I will ask if what isn't broken should be fixed.

I will not be deterred by criticism.

I will not allow "killer messages" to prevent me from pursuing and developing ideas.

> As is our confidence, so is our capacity.
> —WILLIAM HAZLITT

• **Try reflecting on your good points,** your strengths, and those qualities which raise your self-esteem, as another way of creative affirmation. Take five minutes and entertain only positive thoughts about yourself. At first you will find it difficult not to think negative thoughts. Try to resist these and focus only on positive ones.

Still another way to affirm yourself is to write a fantasy résumé for your ideal self. Try to write it in your mind first. Fantasize as much as you'd like about your skills and qualifica-

> If you would create something, you must be something.
> —GOETHE

tions but make the job one you would really like to have. Where did this person (that is, you) go to school? With whom did you study? How many languages do you speak? What special computer competencies do you have? What kind of communication skills do you have? Visualize yourself going through the interview. How confident are you? How do you talk? How do you ask questions? Answer questions?

Facing Fears

Face fears.   One of the greatest obstacles to creative thinking is fear. The creative thinker needs to face and manage fear. Fear of criticism is perhaps the major fear. Hearing others say, "That's a dumb idea" or "We tried that before and it didn't work" or, even worse, "You can't be serious" is frightening. Related to this is the fear of failure or fear of making a public mistake. This fear is often combined with the fear of losing face, of damaging your reputation. No one wants to be criticized publicly and yet new ideas and new insights will invariably be criticized. Consider Fulton's steamboat ("Fulton's folly") or the Louisiana Purchase (many Americans thought the price of less than 3 cents an acre was wasted money), or a heavier than air flying machine (impossible, it would never work). William Miller, in *The Creative Edge*, offers other examples. For instance, the head of the patent office, Charles Duells, said in 1899 "Everything that can be invented has been invented" while the head of Warner Brothers, Harry Warner, claimed in 1927 that no one really wants to hear actors talk. It's helpful to keep such examples in mind and perhaps to respond to criticism with one or two such examples.

And, don't be afraid of your intuition. Use it. Intuition is based on your past experiences, thoughts, and feelings. So, use this knowledge and at least explore your intuitions, think about them, mentally assess the consequences of pursuing them. You don't have to follow these intuitive feelings; just think about them.

Take risks. The creative thinker is willing to fail and realizes that it is through failure that really important insights and improvements often come. A good case in point is the failure of 3M to produce a bra that was made of nonwoven fibers. The shape of the bra, however, led them to develop the disposable surgical and safety masks—an idea that quickly became a multi-million dollar business (Rich 1984).

As you approach these creative thinking techniques, do realize that these are not substitutes for knowledge and competence in the field in which you are working. In fact, as stressed earlier, an in-depth knowledge of the field is assumed as a basic foundation for being able to develop new and useful ideas and to implement them in the real world.

A great irony of human thinking is our simultaneous love for new ideas and our reactive fear of them.
—**KARL ALBRECHT**

Creativity comes from trust. Trust your instinct.
—**RITA MAE BROWN**

People have to make themselves predictable, because otherwise the machines get angry and kill them.
—**GREGORY BATESON**

That Uncreative Tie

Although the standard dress for the male executive is a suit and tie, some research shows that wearing a tie may not be a very good idea (Lanagan and Watkins 1987, Stine and Bewares 1994). There is some evidence to indicate that the tie can actually restrict the flow of blood to the brain, resulting in impaired thinking. For example, it has been shown that the response time of those wearing ties was longer (that is, slower) than the response time of those not wearing ties.

Creative Visualization

You are today where your thoughts have brought you; you will be tomorrow where your thoughts take you.
—JAMES ALLEN

Creative visualization is a technique for giving you insight into how you might achieve a goal. It involves visualizing what it would be like to achieve your goal. Let's say, for example, that you want to be taken more seriously on your job. Using creative visualization, you would picture what it would be like if you were taken seriously. Or, go one better: Visualize everyone on the job—even the president and CEO—taking you so seriously that

Everything in the world is created by what you think.
—OPRAH WINFREY

they refuse to make a move without first seeking your advice.

• **Try creative visualization** with this very example as you think about each of the following questions:

How do you feel?

How do you act? How do you walk? How do you sit?

How do you dress?

What does your voice sound like?

How do you talk with colleagues?

How do you spend your lunch time?

How self-confident do you feel? How is your self-esteem?

A picture is an intermediate something between a thought and a thing.
—SAMUEL T. COLERIDGE

Now, think of how this picture of yourself as goal-achiever differs from the picture of yourself at the present time. What are the differences? Might you appear to lack self-confidence? To not believe in yourself? Might you be communicating this self-image to others?

You might also want to try this technique on any number of other problems, for example, asking for a date, giving a great public speech, interviewing for that ideal job, or asking for a raise. You might also find it valuable to actually build creative visualization time into your schedule—five minutes in the morning and five minutes in the afternoon can often provide needed and productive breaks.

There is nothing either good or bad but thinking makes it so.
—SHAKESPEARE, HAMLET

Exercise for the Brain

Although we normally think of exercise as something useful for the body, it's also useful to the brain (Thayer 1988, Stine and Bewares 1994). For example, exercise increases the amount of oxygen that goes to the brain and

---

that increases mental activity. Similarly, exercise releases endorphins which has the effect of lessening many of the negative emotions like depression or anger.

Thus, when you meet a creative block or when negative feelings get in the way of clear thinking, try exercising. The increase in the oxygen supply to the brain and the release of endorphins are likely to give you a creative thinking boost.

The Director's Chair

If I look confused it's because I'm thinking.

—SAM GOLDWYN

This technique places you in the director's chair and stimulates you to create a movie of any aspect on which you want to focus: your life, your problem, your interpersonal relationship, a group meeting you'll lead, your professional development, a negotiation session you'll participate in, or a proposal you want to present.

The steps are simple:

1. Title and focus your movie. What aspect do you want to focus on?
2. Assemble the cast. Who will be in this movie? Do you want to delete certain characters who would normally be a part of the scenario? Do you want to add new characters? How will you define the characters?
3. Write the script.

4. Rehearse the actors. Tell the actors what you want them to say. What attitudes should they hold and reveal? What personality should they project?
5. Action; direct the actors to play their parts as you wish.

The value of this experience is that it helps you focus on specific aspects of, say, your professional development, that you might want to change, or on your professional goals or on the training you need. Since you're the director, you can have the movie go in any direction you'd like.

My favorite thing is to go where I've never been.
—DIANE ARBUS

• **Try taking the director's chair** and create a movie of your professional life. What would you title it? What kind of music would you hear as the title and credits flash on the screen? Who will be a part of this life? Can you name the specific people? Can you identify the types of people? What will they look like? What would their roles be? What is the general story line? Can you summarize the film—as it might appear in a synopsis in the movie guide? What rehearsal suggestions will you give to the actors? How would you want them to act? Remember this is your movie, your life, so you can visualize it in any way you'd like.

Never be afraid to sit awhile and think.
—LORRAINE HANSBERRY

At another time try focusing specifically on yourself as a communicator. Direct a movie that focuses on your life as a communicator—intrapersonally, interpersonally, socially, and publicly—or on some specific part of your communication life. For example, consider directing a movie of such situations as these:

♦ your next job interview
♦ your next public speech

Think before you think!
—STANISLAW J. LEC

- your next serious relationship argument
- asking for a raise or a promotion
- asking someone for a date

Mindfulness

In your text, mindfulness is discussed as a skill for thinking about how to apply the other skills of communication such as empathy or openness. But, mindfulness is also a tool for encouraging creative thinking. Becoming mindful of your behaviors, thinking consciously about your behaviors, is a good way of gaining another perspective on these perhaps habitual behaviors—things you do because you've always done them that way. Ellen Langer (1989), who developed this concept, offers several suggestions for increasing mindfulness:

- Be open to new information; even if it contradicts your most firmly held stereotypes. This may not be as easy as it sounds. It is often very difficult to listen openly and fairly to ideas that contradict cherished beliefs or attitudes.

- Be open to different points of view. This will help you avoid the tendency to blame outside forces for your negative behaviors ("The questions were unfair" or as comedian Flip Wilson used to say, "The devil made me do it") and internal forces for the negative behaviors of others ("Pat didn't study," "Pat isn't very bright"). Be willing to see your own and others' behaviors from a variety of perspectives.

- Beware of relying too heavily on first impressions. Treat your first impressions as tentative, as hypotheses, not conclusions. The creative thinker is especially aware that there are many answers to a given problem. The answer found first may not be the best one and so he or she is always looking for new and different ways of solving a problem. But, the creative thinker also realizes that at some point thinking needs to give way to action and a decision has to be made (see deBono 1991 for a creative guide to action).

♦ Create and re-create categories. See an object, event, or person as belonging to a wide variety of categories. Avoid storing in your memory an image of a person, for example, with only one specific label. If you do, you will have difficulty recategorizing or relabeling your image of this person. But, people do change and it's essential that we recategorize and relabel on a regular basis. Next is an exercise that explains this important notion more fully and also gives you practice in starting to create and re-create categories.

> Ignorance is not innocence, but sin.
> —ROBERT BROWNING

• **Try creating categories.** Working alone or in small groups, try to create as many categories as you can from the list of 30 items presented below. Each category must contain at least three items. For example, one category might be things that fly which could include the airplane, bee, helicopter, mosquito, and parakeet. A less obvious category might be "things you moisten" and would include the envelope, the postage stamp, wallpaper, razor, bologna, and window. Try to share these categories with others. It'll give you a quick appreciation for the added perspectives that can be brought to bear on a concept by seeing it categorized in widely different ways.

> You see, but you do not observe.
> —SHERLOCK HOLMES

$10 bill	fax machine	parakeet	telephone
airplane	hearing aid	pen	television set
bee	helicopter	pocket knife	transparent tape
bologna	ice cream	postage stamp	wall calendar
camera	microphone	razor	wallpaper
dictionary	milk	ruler	window
envelope	mosquito	scissors	
eye glasses	paper clip	screw driver	

Here's another set of items—this one focusing on communication. Again, create as many different categories as you can:

adaptors	criticism	jargon
affect displays	culture	listening
ambiguity	denotation	love
apprehension	dialogue	markers
argumentativeness	empathy	monologue
attitude	equity	noise
attraction	ethnocentrism	openness
audience	excuse	pauses
belief	feedback	redundancy
censorship	friendship	self-disclosure
channel	game	sexist language
competence	gossip	silence
confidence	I-messages	stereotype
conflict	indirect speech	style
connotation	intensional	territoriality
conversation	orientation	touching
credibility	interaction	you-messages
	management	

The categories you created (and those created by others) should make it clear that a single item can be a member of lots of categories. Creating and recreating categories enables you to develop greater flexibility and not get locked into one way of seeing things. It can help you see that the item (person or event) can also fit into lots of different categories. For example, this ability allows you to see a screwdriver, not only in the category of tools, but also in the category of door stops, can openers, paperweights, nail cleaners, garden implements, electricity current testers, and hole punchers.

> I exist because I think.
> —JEAN-PAUL SARTRE

These examples should make it clear that the meaning of an object or concept is greatly dependent on the way you categorize it and the labels you give it. Realize too that there is a tendency to categorize people into very few categories with the result that we may fail to recognize that any one person may be a member of many categories. Thus, for example, a professor is seldom thought of as also belonging potentially to the category of athletes, musicians, politicians, chess players, or painters. The fewer the categories you have for a person, the less you'll be able to appreciate the multi-dimensionality of this person.

Sens-ational Thinking

A technique recommended by many creative thinking experts (for example, Wujec 1994, von Oech 1990, McGartland 1994, Higgins 1994) is to look at your problem from the perspective of the five senses, a technique easily remembered by our somewhat bizarre name, Sens-ational Thinking. This technique is especially help-

> It is the province of knowledge to speak, and it is the privilege of wisdom to listen.
> —OLIVER WENDELL HOLMES, JR.

Traveling round the world opened up my ears.
—RAY CHARLES

ful in getting in touch with the emotional dimension of a problem. But, it can also help you develop ideas for many problems encountered in business, education, science, and so on. Sens-ational thinking involves allowing yourself to sense the situation/problem/product from the perception of sight, sound, smell, touch, and taste, and is especially effective when it is totally nonverbal. Although this will be difficult, try developing your ability to sense without words.

You probably use this type of thinking when you are deciding between say, two places to go on a Saturday night. You may, for example, picture each of the possibilities in your mind and ask yourself which seems (feels, looks) like the better choice. Sens-ational thinking somewhat formalizes this very natural process. The result or object is to simply gain an additional perspective on

They never taste who always drink; They always talk who never think.

—MATTHEW PRIOR

a decision or problem. Because we've been taught not to trust our feelings, you may have to practice this type of thinking—teaching yourself that you can learn a great deal through all your senses.

• **Try sens-ational thinking** by recalling a specific problem, issue, or unexplained feeling (perhaps deciding between two cars, two job offers, or two elective courses) and ask yourself a variety of sens-ational questions. Following are some specific problems. Try sens-ational thinking to give added insight and additional perspectives by selecting one of these problems (or one of your own) and asking the questions presented below (and others of your own creation):

Speech . . . is an invention of man's to prevent him from thinking.

—HERCULE POIROT

♦ How can I plan the perfect date?

- How can I say "I'm sorry"?
- How can I hold the interest and attention of my audience?
- How can I get my child to be more considerate of others?
- How can I set up an ideal classroom for fourth grade children?
- How can I design a more effective cover for the new vegetarian cookbook?

In much of your talking, thinking is half murdered.

—KAHIL GIBRAN

Visual Sense

What does it look like? What is its visualize image? How might you draw it? Does it have color? Design? How big is it? What's its shape?

Auditory Sense

How does it sound? If it were music, what type of music would it be? Is it noisy or melodious? Is it monotonous or varied? Predictable or exciting?

Olfactory Sense

What does it smell like? Would you call it a scent or an odor? Are the smells reminiscent of other smells?

Kinesthetic Sense

What does it feel like? Is it smooth or rough? Pleasant or unpleasant?

Gustatory Sense

What does it taste like? Is it salty? Sour? Sweet? Bitter?

The Unconscious Knows

Much of knowledge resides in the unconscious. For example, as speakers of English you would know that to form a plural for the never-before seen "word" *dag*, you would add a -z sound, to form a plural for *dat* you would add an -s sound, and to form the plural for *datch* you would add an -ez sound. But, you would probably not be able to state the rule that you were following in forming these plurals of "words" you never saw before (Berko 1957).

Consider another example. Students were asked to press a button corresponding to where an X would appear on a computer screen (Goleman 1992, Stine and Bewares 1994). They were offered a reward of $100 if they could identify the system of rules governing where the X would appear on the screen. Now, the interesting thing about this was that the students could not state the system of rules governing the appearance of the X. But, they were able to predict where the X would appear next. The system of rules that they had to follow to predict where the X would appear was apparently in their unconscious or at least below the level of conscious awareness.

Creative thinking techniques are designed to allow you to tap into this reservoir of knowledge.

Travels in Time and Space

Gaining a perspective from a different time or from a different place is often helpful in getting a different picture of your problem (Wujec 1988). Use the Time Machine and the Groundhog, the Deer, and the Hawk techniques to acquire these different perspectives.

The *Time Machine* is a helpful technique for viewing problems because all problems, all events, all communications, have a time dimension. Everything occurs in time. And while the event does not change—it occurred once—your memory of it often will. Similarly, the meaning you give to the event will change. So, it is often helpful to think about how time influences any given problem. Let's say, for example, that you are passed over for a promotion. You need to decide what you're going to do about this—if anything.

> Time and space are the only forms of thought.
> —EDITH NESBITT

The Time Machine helps you to gain a temporal perspective on this problem. So, get in the Time Machine and fast forward, three years. What will this event (being passed up for promotion) mean to you three years from now? What will your life be like? Fast forward again, this time 10 years. What will being passed up for promotion mean to you then? Compare your present feelings with what you might be feeling three or ten years from now. Does this give you any insight into your problem? Does it help you decide what you should do? Similarly, you might want to go back in time to think about what happened before you were passed up for promotion.

The *Groundhog, the Deer, and the Hawk* technique is useful when you want to get a different spatial perspective. Say, for example, that you are a decorator. Take the per-

> The empires of the future are the empires of the mind.
> —WINSTON CHURCHILL

spective of the groundhog and look at the room from the bottom up, much as a small child—a technique that decorators of children's rooms would find most enlightening. Take the perspective of the deer and stare at one area, learning as much as you can about this area and then gradually shift to another small area and examine it in detail. Can you see any problems? For example, is one area too sparse and another too crowded? Take the perspective of the hawk and look at the room from the top down; stand on a ladder if you have to.

Management, for example, would do well to see the company and their own operations from different space positions—from the position of the mailroom trainee, from the secretary, from the CEO. What insights do each of these viewpoints give you?

Let's say, for example, that you are a politician running for national office. One of the central issues in your campaign is youth violence. To effectively present your views, you would probably find it helpful to see the problem of youth violence from the point of view of people living in different places. How might the problem be seen by someone living in a large city? A rural town? An isolated farm? For other problems it might be helpful to gain a more global perspective and ask yourself, how the farmer in India, the factory worker in Texas, the machine operator in Greece see the problem?

Tom Wujec in *Pumping Ions* (1988) notes that Steven Spielberg—in trying to figure out how to design the spaceship for *Close Encounters of the Third Kind* stood on his head and viewed the city skyline. And that was the idea for the spaceship—a city upside down. Changing your temporal or spatial perspective may help you gain a fresh view of your surroundings, your problems, and perhaps potentially valuable solutions.

- **Try traveling in time and space** to get different perspectives and ideas on one or more of the questions presented below (or, better, questions of your own choosing). Sharing your responses and insights with others will further illustrate the potential applications of this technique.

- What should I major in?
- How can I design the ideal conference room?
- How does communication fit into my interpersonal and professional lives?
- What would the ideal kitchen look like?
- What kind of field should I enter?
- How can we improve our family communication?
- How might a more efficient work space be designed?
- How can I do better at job interviews?
- What would the ideal nursery school classroom be like?
- How can I become a more effective manager or supervisor?

Surprise!

Philosopher Alfred North Whitehead once remarked that "almost all really new ideas have a certain aspect of foolishness when they are just produced." "Mind surprise," a technique suggested by Robert Olson (1980), capitalizes on this notion of the foolish idea.

In using this technique, you develop foolish or ridiculous solutions to a problem and then—once you have these clearly inappropriate solutions—you try to turn them into

All things are at odds when God lets a thinker loose on this planet.
—EDITH HAMILTON

useful and reasonable possibilities. French author and Nobel prize recipient Albert Camus seemed to have this in mind when he wrote: "All great ideas and all great thoughts have a ridiculous beginning. Great works are often born on a street corner or in a restaurant's revolving door."

• **Try Surprise!**   to help you identify the characteristics of a responsive relationship partner. To do this using the Surprise technique, you might generate such foolish and obviously inappropriate responses as these:

1. Avoid my partner.
2. Eat by myself.
3. Invite other people over without checking first.
4. Talk with colleagues on the phone all evening.

The absurd is the essential concept and the first truth.
—ALBERT CAMUS

Then you examine each of these and try to see what values there might be in changing the suggestions around. Do they stimulate you to think of more reasonable solutions? Here, for example, are some possibilities you might come up with for the four ridiculous solutions noted above.

1. Give my partner space—both psychological and physical.
2. Take my partner to dinner at a great restaurant.
3. Organize a surprise party.
4. Call my partner during the day to say "hello".

It takes a smart man to know he's stupid.
—BARNEY RUBBLE,
"THE FLINTSTONES"

The reasonable suggestions do not have to be the opposite of the ridiculous ones. Just use the ridiculous suggestions to jog your mind into thinking of more realistic and potentially useful alternatives.

Here's another example. You want to consider how you can become a more efficient and more effective student. Here are some ridiculous suggestions:

1. Cut classes.
2. Don't read your textbooks.
3. Don't ask questions in class.
4. Always begin assignments late.

Human salvation lies in the hands of the creatively maladjusted.
—**MARTIN LUTHER KING, JR.**

Using these suggestions as take off points, try to derive potentially useful solutions.

Try another exercise. Start with a general question and develop ridiculous solutions and then derive reasonable ones from them. Here are a few general questions you might want to use (or you can develop your own):

♦ How can I plan more exciting dates?
♦ How can I better resolve interpersonal conflicts?
♦ How can I become a better writer?
♦ How can I spend my time more productively?
♦ How can I earn more money?

Puzzling Assumptions

This is a puzzle you've probably seen many times, but it helps illustrate a very important principle. The objective is to connect all 9 dots with 4 straight continuous lines;

---

there can be no breaks between your 4 lines. Try it for a few minutes before reading on.

```
●   ●   ●

●   ●   ●

●   ●   ●
```

If you had difficulty solving this "simple" problem, you probably added the restriction that the dots represented a square and that your lines could not extend beyond this square. With this assumption, the problem becomes impossible to solve. But, once you abandon this assumption, the problem becomes simple. See the answer on page 106.

This puzzle illustrates the need to become aware of your assumptions and to discard those that get in the way of creative problem solving. In fact, you can look at many of the techniques presented here as ways of circumventing common—but debilitating—assumptions.

The Abstraction Ladder

A simple but useful idea to gain a somewhat different perspective on a problem or question is to vary its level of abstraction, to see the problem at a higher and at a lower level of abstraction. For example, if your problem is "How can I write more effective progress reports?" you might gain a different perspective on this by asking questions at higher and at a lower level of abstraction:

With method and logic one can accomplish anything.
—HERCULE POIROT

Higher level of abstraction:
How can I become a more effective writer?
Original question:
How can I write better progress reports?
Lower level of abstraction:
How can I write better openings for these reports?

Notice that the level of abstraction on which you phrase your question influences the types of answers and ideas you generate. Take the first example. The higher level question focuses attention on improving writing in general. Sentence length, active versus passive sentences, direct versus indirect constructions, writing dialogue, and the like are possible areas that this question might suggest. The lower level question, on the other hand, focuses attention on the very specific area of opening paragraphs, and might suggest attention to such areas as previewing summary recommendations, stating pertinent questions in an opening box, or identifying the objectives of the report.

Here are a few other examples to further illustrate this technique:

Higher level of abstraction:
How can I gain more self control?
Original question:
How can I stick to my diet?
Lower level of abstraction:
How can I reduce the sugar in my diet?

Higher level of abstraction:
>How can I become a more persuasive person?

Original question:
>**How can I persuade this audience?**

Lower level of abstraction:
>How can I gain the audience's attention?

Higher level of abstraction:
>How can I use time more efficiently?

Original question:
>**How can I study more efficiently?**

Lower level of abstraction:
>How can I study history more efficiently?

• **Try developing higher and lower level abstractions** for each of these questions. What different perspectives do these higher and lower abstractions give you?

>How can I become a better relationship partner?
>How can I give up smoking (or any other bad habit)?
>How can I become a better listener?
>How can I become more politically or socially active?
>How can I become a more effective small group leader?
>How can I save more of my income?
>How can I become a better communication student?
>How can I get promoted to supervisor?
>How can I become more popular with my peers?
>How can I increase my credibility in public speaking?

Similarities and Differences

Identifying similarities and differences between your situation
and some other situation will often help you see potential problems and perhaps solutions to them. Some organizations, for example, try to identify the similarities and differences between their
company and some other company, for example, the best run company or the most profitable company. So, for
example, they might compare their advertising methods, their mailing system, or their
fringe benefits package with those of their
leading competitor and look for similarities
and differences. Some companies even set
up an imaginary ideal competitor and compare themselves to this ideal (Higgins
1994). By seeing the similarities and differences in this situation,
you can more easily identify any problems with advertising, mailing operations, or benefit packages for workers.

> There is a great difference
> between knowing and
> understanding, you can
> know a lot about something and
> not really understand it.
> **—CHARLES F. KETTERING**

  The practice is often called "benchmarking," and refers to
the use of a comparison point (a real or imagined ideal company,
for example) to help you measure your own degree of excellence
and your own progress toward that goal. Entire books have been
written on benchmarking (see, for example, Gregory Watson's
Strategic Benchmarking (Wiley, 1993). Benchmarking is extensively used in business where a corporation or department is compared with some ideal or best-run organization. But, it can also be
used to compare your family, your relationships with your children, or your class with idealized situations. Many people compare their romantic relationships with idealized relationships in
literature, in films, and in soap operas without realizing perhaps
that they are engaging in fairly sophisticated creative thinking.

The cleverly expressed opposite of any generally accepted idea is worth a fortune to somebody.
—**GEORGE FRANCIS FITZGERALD**

• **Try seeing similarities and differences** between concepts; it's an excellent way to gain new perspectives and new ideas. Here, for example, are pairs of communication concepts. How are they connected? What do they have in common? How do they differ? For example, for the first comparison *(feedback* and *feedforward)* you might note among the similarities that both are types of messages, both may be verbal or nonverbal or both, and both may contradict or reinforce the regular message. Among the differences you might note that one comes before and one comes after the regular message, one is listener initiated and one is speaker initiated, and one comments on a message already given and one comments on a message to be given.

1. feedback and feedforward
2. gestures and color
3. words and touch
4. thinking and facial expression
5. conversation and public speaking
6. hearing aids and clothing
7. listening and perception
8. speaker and listener
9. cultural context and message
10. interpersonal relationship and noise

One of the categories on the television game show, "Wheel of Fortune" is "?" where the words to be guessed all have another word (designated by "?") in common. Recently, for example, the cue words prefaced by a "?" were *pastry*, *kiss*, and *accent*. The missing word—for an extra $500—was "French." The Remote Associates test (Mednick 1962) works in a similar way and is one of the tests used to study creativity. This test, which focuses on your ability to detect similarities, presents you with three items for which you must supply a word that goes with all three items.

- **Try identifying the remote associates** —the word each triad has in common— before turning to the answers on page 106.

1. pop, crackers, jerk
2. jacket, fever, brick road
3. tennis, lamp, cloth
4. starved, sick, triangle
5. set, guide, station
6. jewelry, cardboard, pencil
7. sky, denim, heaven
8. lie, lightning, sale
9. drinking, magnifying, water
10. ink, river, rose
11. doctor, center, emergency
12. health, home, automobile
13. veins, web, bite
14. high, department, arm
15. high, business, boarding
16. kitchen, pool, conference
17. business, playing, credit
18. bath, tea, conference
19. brain, winter, barn
20. back, front, open
21. entry, concert, lecture
22. tee, sweat, dress
23. pig, fountain, bull
24. couch, white, sweet
25. cover, jacket, bag
26. Waterloo, Brooklyn, dental
27. base, high, debutante
28. bird, school, road
29. jacket, cover, page
30. window, frame, postcard

Exceptional Analysis

Exceptional analysis is a useful technique when you are confronted by a generalization, statement of folk wisdom, or general rule that you want to go beyond (Koberg and Bagnall 1976a, b; Michalko 1991). For example, in the face of the enormous number of research findings that you will encounter in college and in your professional career, it may be helpful to take time out and ask about the exceptions. After all, even research results reporting that "the vast majority of those surveyed" or "ninety-five percent of the subjects"—and few research findings are that conclusive—still don't account for everyone.

In a similar way, each culture maintains it's own system of "truths" that are often true but in some cases may not be true. For example, members of many Asian cultures, influenced by Confucian principles, believe that "the protruding nail gets pounded down" (in the words of Confucius) and are therefore not likely to voice disagreement with the majority at a group meeting. Americans, influenced by the belief that "the squeaky wheel gets the grease," are more likely to voice disagreement or to act in ways different from other group members. Mindless adherence to either principle is probably not a very good idea and a search for exceptions might prove helpful. By looking at the exceptions to the rule, you will often gain a different perspective on an issue.

> You know my method. It is founded upon the observance of trifles.
> **—SHERLOCK HOLMES**

• **Try exceptional analysis.** Here, for example, are examples of generalizations that we often hear but which we seldom examine for exceptions. In looking over the list, ask yourself if you believe these statements and if so, on the basis of what evidence? Then, ask yourself what are some actual or easily imagined exceptions to the rule. For example, to the statement "No one likes a smart aleck" you might add "unless the smart aleck is a popular stand-up comic." To the statement "Money has nothing to do with happiness" you might add "unless you're comparing those above and those below the poverty line; in these cases money does made a difference. Those above the poverty line are significantly happier than those below."

A happy worker is a productive worker.
A stitch in time saves nine.
Absence makes the heart grow fonder.
Admit your mistakes.
Always be supportive of those you love.
An ounce of prevention is worth a pound of cure.
Be positive in conversation.
Beauty is in the eye of the beholder.
Beauty is only skin deep.
Birds of a feather flock together.
Democratic leaders are best.
Empathize with your relationship partner.
Haste makes waste.
Honesty is the best policy.
Honor thy father and thy mother.
It is better to have loved and lost than never to have loved at all.
Like father like son. Like mother like daughter.
Money has nothing to do with happiness.
Never reveal everything about yourself.
Never betray a confidence.
No one likes a smart aleck.
One who hesitates is lost.
Opposites attract.
People make their own luck.
Real men don't cry.
Small groups are more creative than individuals.
The squeaky wheel gets the grease.
The protruding nail gets pounded down.
The apple doesn't fall far from the tree.
When in doubt say nothing.

When in Rome do as the Romans do.

Work hard.

You can catch more flies with honey than you can with vinegar.

Shaving with Ockham's Razor

This principle comes from the writings of William of Ockham, a fourteenth century English philosopher. The idea is that the best explanation or solution or theory is that which is simplest; it is that which requires the least number of assumptions. Thus, when evaluating two or three or four potential solutions, Ockham's razor would tell you to select the one that is simplest. Procter and Gamble extended the use of Ockham's razor in their policy of simplification; they tried to discover what was not necessary to their goals and what, therefore, could be eliminated (Olson 1980). The technique involves asking three questions:

- Can we eliminate it entirely?
- Can we eliminate it partially?
- Can we substitute a simpler/lower cost alternative?

   Another way to use Ockham's razor is to look at a problem—for example, when everything seems to be going wrong—and shave off all the incidentals that get in the way of a clear view of the problem. Or you can shave away all the pieces of the problem over which you have no control and focus your energies on what you can do to make your situation better. In this way the problem may be reduced to more managable proportions that can be easily dealt with.

Attribute Listing and Reversal

Attribute listing and reversal is a commonly used creative thinking technique (for example, vanGundy 1992, Wujec 1994, Miller 1994, Higgins 1994). It is designed to help you think differently about an object or problem, forcing you to re-examine things that you usually take for granted—as somehow natural and unchangeable. The technique consists of listing the qualities or attributes of an object and then reversing or changing them in any way imaginable.

> I can always be distracted by love, but eventually I get horny for my creativity.
> **—GILDA RADNER**

Let's take the common ordinary ruler as an example. The one on my desk is made of wood, 12 inches long, 1 inch wide, one eighth of an inch thick, with markings every sixteenth of an inch. This is essentially the listing process. In the next stage you would change or reverse the attributes. Notice that we can look at each attribute as asking an implicit question, namely "What else can a ruler be made of?" "Can it be longer or shorter than 12 inches?" "What are some other widths that the ruler might be?" And so on.

You might construct a simple two column table with the attributes of the ruler on the left and the potential changes on the right. It might look something like Table 2.

• **Try attribute listing and reversal** either alone or in a group. Try to develop a new, potentially marketable product. Use one of the following items or try one of your own:

CDs	diskette caddy
belts	book marker
tool box	magnifying glass
staple machine	eye glass case
lamp	alarm clock

Table 2. Attribute listing table.

Attribute	Change, Reversal, Modification
wood	plastic, metal, paper, cardboard
solid	with holes for looseleaf, with cutouts of geometric figures for stencils, with smiling face cut outs, collapsible
12 inches long	6 inches, 8 inches, 10 inches, 14 inches, 16 inches, 24 inches
1 inch wide	1/2 inch, 1 1/2 inches, 2 inches, 3 inches
markings every sixteenth of an inch	markings every 32nds of an inch, every inch, every half inch
blank on back	commonly used information such as often called phone numbers, weights and measures, first aid information, commonly misspelled words, common spelling or grammatical rules, common phrases in a variety of foreign languages

Similar to attribute listing and reversal is morphological analysis (Van Gundy 1993, Miller 1987). Morphological analysis is a technique for creating new ideas such as new products, or for revising existing ones. It is especially useful when your problem is one that has clearly defined attributes that can be easily identified and listed. It thus works best when you are dealing with a concete object such as a product or a service.

> It is completely unimportant. That is why it is so interesting.
>
> —HERCULE POIROT

You begin morphological analysis with a product and an objective. Let's take a doll as an example, and creating new types of dolls as our objective. The first step is to identify the major parts of the product and arrange these into columns. In the case of the doll you might have columns for materials, gender, clothing, age, and species.

CREATIVE THINKING TECHNIQUES

Your second step would be to identify the components of each of these major parts and list these within the appropriate column. For example, under materials you would list all the materials that a doll could possibly be constructed of. You comparison chart would begin to look something like Table 3. Note that many of the items can be further subdivided, for example, the varieties of metals, woods, and papers could be identified.

DOLL

Materials	Gender	Clothing	Age	Species
metal	male	historical	premie	human
wood	female	contemporary	infant	alien
paper	male/female	futuristic	baby	superhero
plastic		ethnic	child	animal
cloth			adolescent	angel
clay			teenager	TV character
			adult	
			senior citizen	

Table 3. Simplified morphological analysis table.

Of course, you could create finer distinctions by subdividing many of the items listed here and instead of metal, for example, list the specific types of metal: tin, copper, steel, gold, silver, and so on. It is generally best to be as specific as possible. Whenever a category can be subdivided, do it. You can always throw out the ones you don't want to use at some later time.

Your third step is to scan the chart and identify products that are possible—but not necessarily worthwhile. Thus, for example, you might imagine an infant angel doll that is both male and female, composed of cloth, and dressed in various ethnic clothing.

Or you might consider a doll that is a female teenage superhero dressed in historically accurate clothing for different periods of time and made of cardboard.

Of course, this example does not exhaust all the categories that you could and should use. For example, lets say you also included the category of size and you noted that dolls could range from, say, one inch to 7 or 8 feet tall. With this as a category and with, say, your metals broken down into various types, you might envision miniature dolls dressed in historically accurate clothing. From this you might think of making the dolls into jewelry. From this you might design jewelry dolls to match the more traditional dolls. Two types of dolls could then be sold: the traditional dolls plus the jewelry dolls. The parent might wear the jewelry doll while the child carries the "regular" doll.

- **Try morphological analysis.** Select a product of your own and try to develop either a spin-off or similar product. If you prefer, select one of these general products for your morphological analysis: trading cards, desk lamp, screen-saver, birdhouse, television situation comedy, magazine, appointment book, college textbooks, bulletin board, souvenier for the baseball world series games, telephone, greeting card, book cover for a series of romance novels set in the year 3000, a calendar, a coat rack. Your objective is to develop a new, potentially marketable product.

Take advantage of the ambiguity in the world. Look at something and think about what else it might be.
—ROGER VON OECH

Metaphors and Similes

"The metaphor," said Jose Ortega y Gasset, "is probably the most fertile power possessed by man." Metaphor and simile are among the most powerful of all creative thinking techniques.

Metaphors and similes are comparisons; they state that an association exists between the items being compared. Similes use "like" or "as" in stating the comparisons ("He was hungry as a lion") whereas metaphors do not ("He was a regular lion in the mornings"). The *Metaphors and Similes* technique is based on the idea that by comparing two things that are similar in some respects and different in other respects, you can gain an interesting perspective on the concept or problem (Koberg and Bagnall 1976a, b; Higgins 1994; McGartland 1994).

You can use metaphors and similes in a variety of ways. You might, for example, simply ask yourself how your problem is like a tree, cloud, rain, a $3 bill, lion, child, river, sitcom, or work of fine art. Select items on your desk, on TV, or in a magazine.

Or, you can think of a topic, say, sports, and ask how your problem is like a game of basketball, tennis, football, golf, and so on. In a group situation, if each member contributes one metaphor, a wide variety of perspectives on your problem will be quickly generated. Discussion can be directed at elaborating on each contribution, on selecting those metaphors that seem particularly true or those that embody assumptions which are untrue, on providing an example for each metaphor proposed.

You can use metaphors and similes to analyze your own situation and compare it with your ideal. For example, using a transportation metaphor/simile, "Mornings with Pat are like a sports

A trite word is an overused word which has lost its identity like an old coat in a second-hand shop. The familiar grows dull and we no longer see, hear, or taste it.

—ANAIS NIN

car—fast and furious; but my ideal would be a horse and buggy—slow and easy."

Roger von Oech (1990) suggests using metaphors containing actions and suggests such metaphors as "starting a revolution," "putting out a fire," "building a house," "planting a garden," and "conducting an orchestra." You would then ask how your problem is similar to these action metaphors: How is our relationship like starting a revolution? How is writing a book like planting a garden? How is teaching a class like conducting an orchestra?

• **Try to develop metaphors or similes** for the following communication concepts: noise, feedback, context of communication, gestures, touch, eye movements, interpersonal communication, interviewing, small group discussions, conversation, intercultural communication, and public speaking.

If you're ready to develop more metaphors and similes, try composing them for such relationship concepts as: my ideal romantic partner, interpersonal attraction, friendship, love, family, sibling rivalry, courtship, relationship dissolution, and conflict.

Creating a Masterpiece or Doodling

Research on brain function shows that it takes just as much energy to create a masterpiece as it does to doodle (Gevins 1981, Stine and Bewares 1994) Records of brain waves from people engaged in creating a serious work of art and those who were just doodling shows that the level of energy was the same. So, if you want to give your brain a workout, you might just as well set yourself the task of creating a masterpiece.

Checklists

To a great mind, nothing is little.
—**SHERLOCK HOLMES**

Checklists are common in all walks of life and are a commonly recommended creative thinking tool (Higgins 1994). Prepared checklists are used for shopping, evaluating leadership performance or a nursery school program, for checking out perspective mates or job applicants, publishing a magazine, preparing a party, and for just about any activity that requires you to consider a series of items. Checklists are used by automotive engineers and repair mechanics to discover vehicle problems, by doctors examining a patient, by a quality control engineer examining the production of aspirin, by the social worker who investigates family conditions, by the communication consultant who audits the communications of an organization. And they are used in many textbooks to stimulate the reader to review the major concepts and skills learned.

Checklists are valuable in helping to make sure, as you review the steps in a process, that you have left nothing out. They can also help you to identify all the essential steps in a process so you'll be able to check to see that you've progressed as you should have. Checklists help you review and help you to organize and prioritize your agenda items.

Checklists are also standard tools in creative thinking. Checklists help you review a list of possibilities systematically and ensure that important elements will not be overlooked or neglected. Checklists are also used extensively in communication. For example, let's say you were preparing a public speech and you wanted to evaluate your preparation and see if what you had done will prove satisfactory. To do this, you might use a checklist. Table 4 provides an example of a checklist you might use in evaluating an introduction to a public speech. Once prepared, the checklist would be available for all your speeches.

In a similar manner, checklists might be prepared for just about any activity that involves a series of decisions to accomplish them, such as leading a meeting, teaching a class, creating an advertisement, interviewing a potential employee, planning a vacation, or saving to buy a house.

Table 4.

A Sample Checklist for a Speech Introduction

The Speech Introduction Checklist

Does my introduction gain attention? Have I effectively made use of the techniques for gaining attention?

> Use a quotation?
> Tell a humorous story?
> Ask a question?
> Refer to audience members?
> Refer to recent happenings?
> Use an illustration or dramatic story?
> Stress importance of the topic?
> Use audiovisual aids?
> Tell the audience to pay attention?
> Refer to yourself?
> Refer directly to the topic?
> Cite a little known fact or statistic?

Does my introduction establish a connection among myself, my topic, and my audience? Have I used the effective means of connection?

Establish my credibility?
Refer to others present?
Refer to the occasion?
Express my pleasure in speaking?
Compliment the audience?
Express similarities with the audience?

Does my introduction preview my topic for the audience? Have I used the effective means for orienting an audience?

Give a detailed preview?
Identify my goal?
Introduce the topic and its importance?

Does my introduction avoid the major common faults?

Do I apologize?
Do I make hollow promises?
Do I rely on gimmicks?

• **Try using checklists** by having a group of five or six select a common topic problem and independently prepare checklists. After each person feel comfortable with her or his checklist, the lists should be pooled and one master composite list constructed. Try this for any topic you feel would lend itself to checklist thinking, or use one of these:

♦ preparing a party for 50 guests
♦ interviewing for a job
♦ saving for retirement

- preparing for a department meeting
- deciding on and buying a car
- organizing a conference
- preparing a company newsletter
- preparing a calendar for a hypothetical company or for your class
- dressing for success
- preparing an AIDS Awareness Day at your college or place of work

When something needs to be painted it lets me know.
—LUIS FRANGELLA

Altercasting

A story is told of a woman who took her very young child shopping during the crowded holiday season. As they went from store to store and department to department, the child became more and more irritable and cried and complained. After about an hour of such shopping, the child's shoelace came untied and the mother bent down to retie it. As she bent down she saw the world from the point of view of the child. Able to see only the legs and shoes of people and none of the holiday displays, she understood the child's frustration (Hanks, Belliston, and Edwards 1978). Without any planning, this mother exchanged places with the child and saw the world from the child's perspective. This is the basic process involved in altercasting—to exchange roles with another person.

In communication we talk of altercasting as a conversational strategy whereby you ask another person to assume the role of someone else. So, you might ask a friend "What would you do if you were the manager?" or "How would you handle your kids if you just won the lottery?" Altercasting is a way of structuring the conversation and steering the listener into a particular perspective or role.

Altercasting is also a powerful creative thinking tool, similar to *Galileo and the Ghosts* and *The Professionals* which follow. Putting yourself into the frame of mind of someone else can often bring considerable insights.

Actors have long used this technique to help them better understand a particular part they will play. Thus, the actor playing an athlete, for example, may find it profitable to actually play the sport and interact with other athletes. The procedure helps the actor understand the nature of the athlete and the sport by actually becoming an athlete, or at least coming as close as possible. Put differently, the actor hopes to get ideas about playing the athlete from this role playing. And that is basically the nature of this technique. Georges Simenon's detective, Inspector Maigret, used this technique in solving crimes. "I shall know the murderer," noted Maigret, "when I know the victim well."

To help you better understand another person, consider using altercasting and playing the role of the other person. For example, if you are a real estate sales representative, it would help if you placed yourself in the role of the home buyer and perhaps even went through the process of looking for a home as a would-be buyer.

♦ **Try altercasting** in the following situations.

  ♦ An advertiser concerned with developing a package for a new cereal, toothpaste, or detergent.

  ♦ A designer for a foodstore wants to increase sales, despite two new supermarkets in the area.

  ♦ A new teacher wants to be a great teacher.

- A company manager supervises twenty culturally diverse men and women.
- A parent whose child is often truant.
- A supervisor with overly slow trainees.

Altercasting is also useful when two people want to understand the perspective of the other; each might altercast and play the role of the other. In this **role reversal** you and your romantic partner might each play the part of the other in a mock argument. The reverse role playing allows you to see how your partner sees you and allows your partner to see how you see him or her.

Brain cells

According to Isaac Asimov in *The Brain* (1983; Stine and Benares 1994), at about 21 years of age the brain begins to lose brain cells. In fact, the average brain loses approximately 10,000 brain cells every day. That comes to 3,650,000 cells per year. But, a normal brain with 200 billion cells will hardly notice the loss.

It is interesting to note that management's often subjective impression is that job performance declines with age. However, objective measures show that job performance actually increases as employees grow older (Meer 1986).

In addition, you might try these suggestions for age-proofing yourself offered by Kristin White (1993): "Keep your job. Don't retire. Ever. Stay physically healthy. Become an expert in something—anything. Take up the piano. Take a course in something. Learn to roll with the punches. Do crossword puzzles. Go out with friends or

---

CREATIVE THINKING TECHNIQUES

> find new playmates. Learn French in four years, not four weeks. Turn off the TV. Stock your life with rich experiences of all kinds. Play with toys. Lots of them. Different ones. Skip bingo. Play bridge instead."

Originality consists in thinking for yourself, and not in thinking unlike other people.
—J. FITZJAMES STEPHEN

The Professionals

The Professionals is a useful technique to help you look at a problem and generate a wide variety of perspectives or ways of looking at your problem (cf. von Oech 1990, Higgins 1994). The technique will become more meaningful if you work through a specific problem as you read this. So, begin by selecting a problem, for example: "How can I find a good job?" "How should we promote our new salt-free cereal?" "How can our college heighten AIDS awareness?" Next, take such diverse professionals as these and consider how each of them might approach your problem:

Reporter: Who was involved? What happened? Where did it happen? When did it happen? Why did it happen? To whom did it happen?

Detective: What was the means? What was the motive? Was there opportunity? Is there an alibi or excuse or extenuating circumstance?

Physician: What are the symptoms? Possible causes? Potential remedies?

It is of the highest importance in the art of detection to be able to recognize out of a number of facts which are incidental and which vital. Otherwise your energy and attention must be dissipated instead of being concentrated.
—SHERLOCK HOLMES

Chef: What are the ingredients? The amounts? How are they combined?

Lawyer: What is the evidence? What conclusions can be drawn?

A variation is to enlist the perspectives of academics. For example, assume that my question is "How can I write better textbooks?" I might ask the academics and imagine how they might each respond. Visualize yourself asking the same question about textbooks to your professors in history, anthropology, philosophy, science, and management. How would they each respond? Some preliminary thoughts they might suggest are presented in Table 5. In reviewing this table consider the kinds of questions that

Table 5. Ideas Generated by the Academics.

Academics	Sample Questions
Historian	Can you give the books a historical perspective, for example, showing the development of communication through the centuries? Can communication developments be coordinated with historical events and changes?
Anthropologist	Can the books reflect a multiculturalism? Can the books incorporate an awareness of the arbitrariness of rules for communication and behavior?
Philosopher	Can the concept of ethics be integrated with all topics instead of confined to one chapter? Can the books include insights into communication from the great philosophers?
Psychologist	Can the books include insight into the self? Can psychological research on perception be integrated?
Scientist	Can evolutionary theories of relationships be integrated into the relationship chapters? Can the biological bases for gender differences be included?
Management	Can the books prepare students for the demands of business? For leadership positions in organizations?

might be asked by academics in communication? Engineering? Sociology? Music and theatre? Police science?

• **Try thinking with the professionals.**   For example, let's say you are a member of an advertising team charged with the task of developing a multi-million dollar advertising campaign for a new shampoo that not only cleans your hair but also styles it. You might want to first get a clear in-depth view of the product before even beginning to think about specific advertising strategies. If so, the professionals—let's choose the reporter—might prove a useful technique. A response page similar to Table 6 might be prepared. Note that it has columns for each of the questions the reporter would suggest along with more specific questions. Group members would respond to each question (using the more specific questions as guides). A number of ways of dealing with these pages are possible:

1. They may be passed to others for additional comments (like the Add-a-Tag group to be discussed later).

2. They may be submitted to the group's editor or one from outside the group who would compose a composite response with indications of how many people identified any possible answer

3. They may be used as the basis for a general discussion.

   Robert Olson in *The Art of Creative Thinking* recommends a technique similar to the professionals, namely asking people very different from yourself and unrelated and unconnected to your problem. Olson, for example, asked a child: How can I use my time more effectively? The child responded: "eat less." This

Table 6. The Reporter's Questions Applied to Understanding a Product.

Reporter's Questions	Responses
Who? Who would use the shampoo? Who uses shampoo most? Who buys the shampoo? Who styles their hair?	
What? What is the shampoo made of? What color is it? What color should it be? How does it feel? How does it pour?	
Where? Where would the shampoo be sold? Where is it placed in the store? Where is it placed in the home? Where do people style their hair?	
When? When is shampoo used? When is it not used? When do peole style their hair? When do they not bother with styling?	
Why? Why do people shampoo their hair? Why do people not use shampoo? Why do people style their hair? Why do people not style their hair?	
How? How does the shampoo clean your hair? How does it style your hair?	

prompted Olson to think of using lunch time for important business conferences and discussions. A more dramatic example concerns Edwin Land who had just taken a picture of his small daughter. When she asked why she couldn't see the picture right away, Land began thinking of the developments that eventually led him to create the Polaroid camera (Rice 1984).

Galileo and the Ghosts

Roger von Oech, in his creative *A Whack on the Side of the Head*, suggests that you can gain an interesting perspective on a problem by seeing the problem through the eyes of a particular person (also Higgins 1994). Thus, the technique simply involves asking yourself how would Galileo or Einstein or a favorite author or hero see your problem? The technique helps you to see your problem from a different perspective— from the perspective of a scientific genius, an artist, a religious leader, or a military strategist. The technique seems especially appropriate when there is one person whose behavior you want to imitate or emulate—the outstanding sales representative, the CEO, an admired leader. The technique allows you—as Isaac Newton put it, to see further "by standing on the shoulders of giants."

> I do not feel obliged to believe that the same God who has endowed us with sense, reason, and intellect has intended us to forego their use.
> **—GALILEO**

Applied to the area of interpersonal relationships, this technique might also be used to see the problem from the point of view of your romantic partner, your supervisor at work, or your child. This interpersonal ability to see another's perspective can often make the difference between resolving and not resolving a conflict. Think of what a difference it would make if your supervisor or your romantic partner could see the situation as you see it. In fact, the ability to relate to another person depends largely on the ability to take this other person's perspective. Thus, the effective college instructor (and textbook writer) must take the student's perspective into consideration in planning a

> No matter what accomplishments you make somebody helps you.
> **—ALTHEA GIBSON**

lecture, in designing a syllabus, or writing a textbook; the supervisor must take the trainee's perspective into consideration in planning a training program.

Another way of gaining different perspectives—an extension of the one person "Galileo" technique—is to set up a mental "ghost-thinking team," much like executives and politicians have ghostwriters to write their speeches or corporations and research institutes maintain think-tanks. In this ghost-thinking technique, you select a team of four to eight people you admire, for example, historical figures like Aristotle or Picasso or even fictional figures like Wonder Woman or Captain Picard. If you're knowledgeable about philosophy and can distinguish the pragmatists from the idealists from the scholastics, then you might want to set up a philosophical ghost-thinking team so that you can view your problem from the thoughts of philosophers of different schools of thought. If you wish, select instead friends or relatives you admire.

For some purposes, an effective ghost-team might consist of people from very different walks of life who have very different points of view. You then ask yourself—when confronted by a problem or when in need of different perspectives—how each of these people would deal with your problem (see Figure 2). How would they handle this setback? How would they interview for a job? If you wish, visualize yourself and your ghost-thinking team seated around a conference table, in a restaurant having lunch, or jogging in the park. Choose the team members and the settings in any way you would like. Use whatever works for you and change it any time you want.

Here are some examples of possible ghost team members, chosen to illustrate the wide variety of choices at your disposal.

CREATIVE THINKING TECHNIQUES

The questions too are only suggestive of the wide variety of ways you can use your ghost-thinking team.

A s along as you're going to be thinking anyway, think big.

—DONALD TRUMP

- ♦ Charles Darwin, for his thoroughness in research and his rigorously scientific method, reminds me to search for evidence and to ask: What additional information would help me to solve this problem? Where can I get more data? How can I judge what's true or false? How can I separate what is believed to be true from what really is verifiably true?

- ♦ Donald Trump, for his ability to get things done and to make a lot of money, reminds me to assess the situation for potential rewards and costs and to ask: How can I do this more effectively? How can I make money out of this problem?

- ♦ Mother Teresa, for devoting her life to helping others, reminds me to consider the social usefulness of my actions and to ask: What can I do to help those less fortunate than I? How can I make the world a little better place?

- ♦ Erma Bombeck, for seeing the humor in everyday living and for never giving up, reminds me that many of life's situations have a humorous side to them and to ask: What's funny about this situation? If this weren't happening to me, would I be laughing about this? How can I lighten the atmosphere?

- ♦ Martin Luther King, Jr., for having a dream, reminds me to seek justice for all people and in all situations and to ask: How can what I do better promote social justice? What can I do to make this situation benefit other people?

Your ghost-team bombards your problem with perspectives different from your own. In this ghost-thinking technique the team members view your problem from his or her unique perspective. As a result, your perception of the problem will change; the problem becomes a new one or at least a revised one. Your team members then view this new or revised problem. As a result, your perception of the problem changes again. The process continues until you achieve your aim or decide that this technique has yielded all the insight its going to yield.

Figure 2. The Ghost-Team.

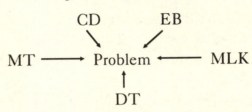

• **Try creating your own initial think-tank,** your own ghost-thinking team. Share your selections with others and then, if you wish, revise your team. Keeping your team from four to eight people will make it manageable and easy to use. You may want to go a step further and begin reading more about these individuals. The more you know about your team members, the more effectively you will be able to use their insights. [Of course, "their insights" are really your insights derived from your interacting with the ideas of these team-members.]

Once you have your ghost-team in place, try asking their advice on one or more of the following questions:

- How should I pursue my education?
- How can I make more money?
- How can I become a more responsive relationship partner?
- How can I become less apprehensive in formal communication situations like interviewing or public speaking?
- How can I increase my assertive communication?

The Quota System

According to the *Guinness Book of Records* (1993), Thomas Alva Edison (1847-1931), inventor of the incandescent light bulb, the microphone, and a motion picture projector, holds the record for the most patents. Either alone or jointly, Edison held 1,093 patents. Part of what made Edison so productive may have been his quota system. Edison made a bargain with himself that every ten days he would develop at least one minor invention and every six months a major one (Michalko 1991). The quota system kept him constantly on the lookout for new ideas and prevented him from becoming satisfied with less than he was capable of giving.

Brainstorming

In its most basic form, creative thinking involves generating lots of ideas quickly and easily and that is exactly what brainstorming is designed to accomplish. *Brainstorming*, developed by Alex Osborn (1957), is a technique for bombarding a problem and generating as many ideas as possible. Osborn created this approach out of the frustra-

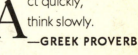

Act quickly, think slowly.
—GREEK PROVERB

tion he encountered in seeing group members agreeing too much and afraid of contradicting their supervisor. Consequently, new ideas were not being developed. Brainstorming was designed to remedy that situation.

Brainstorming is basically a group technique that relies heavily on the contributions of one member stimulating ideas in the minds of the other members. In a group situation, brainstorming is also valuable because it focuses squarely on creative thinking, lessens the inhibition of group members, provides a vivid illustration of the values of cooperative thinking, and builds group members' morale because all members share in the solution of the problem.

The procedures are simple. A problem is selected that is amenable to many possible solutions or ideas ("What can we do to increase worker morale" rather than the much more limiting "Should we have a party to increase worker morale?"). The problem should be phrased as a question that focuses on *one* problem (not "What can we do to improve morale and productivity" but "What can we do to improve morale" *or* "What can we do to improve productivity?").

Inverse Brainstorming

An often productive variation on brainstorming is "inverse brainstorming" (Higgins 1994). Instead of beginning with a problem and trying to find solutions, inverse brainstorming begins with a seemingly normal situation and tries to discover problems. It can be a useful way of anticipating problems and correcting them before they become destructive. It can also be helpful in improving a situation that is really not problematic but that can be made at least a little better.

Ideally, group members are informed of the problem to be brainstormed before the actual session, so they can think about the topic. It is generally recommended that groups consist of between 6 and 12 members—enough to insure that many ideas will be generated, but not so large that members become inhibited. However, I've used brainstorming with an entire class of 30, generating topics for public speeches and information-sharing and problem-solving groups.

The problem should be one that all members can contribute to solving. Depending on the nature of the problem, a group may be composed of persons from the same general background (for example, all sales representatives brainstorming ways to increase orders) or from different backgrounds (for example, sales representatives, advertising managers, marketing analysts, store owners, and product users).

When the group meets, each person contributes as many ideas as he or she can think of. Speed is important. When ideas flow quickly, more ideas will be contributed in the available time and there is likely to be less self-censorship. All ideas are recorded in some way—on a flip-chart, a chalkboard, or tape. During this idea-generating session, four general rules are followed. These rules are applicable to all types of creative thinking and are not limited to brainstorming.

> They never raised a statue to a critic.
> —MARTHA GRAHAM

Don't Criticize

All ideas are recorded. They are not evaluated, nor are they even discussed. Any negative criticism—whether verbal or nonverbal—

is itself criticized by the leader or the members. This is a good general rule to follow in all creative thinking. Allow your idea time to develop before you look for problems with it. At the same time, don't praise the ideas either. All evaluations should be suspended during the brainstorming session.

One of the ways in which you can be on guard against negative criticism is to look out for "idea killers" or "killer messages." These phrases are directed at stopping an idea from being developed, to kill it in its tracks, before it can even get off the ground. Obviously, they need to be avoided in all creative thinking enterprises and especially in brainstorming. Some commonly heard killer messages include:

We tried it before and it didn't work.

It'll never work.

No one would vote for it.

It's too complex.

It's too simple.

It would take too long.

It's too expensive.

It doesn't sound right.

It's not logical.

We don't have the facilities.

It's a waste of time and money.

What we have is good enough.

It won't fly.

It just doesn't fit us.

It's impossible.

Be careful when you hear others say these phrases to you, when you say them to others, and especially when you say them to yourself. These killer messages effectively stifle further explanation, elaboration, extension, and all the processes that can help to develop a germ of an idea into a truly great one.

Strive for Quantity

Linus Pauling, Nobel prize winner for chemistry (1954) and Peace (1962) once said, "The best way to have a good idea is to have lots of ideas." This second rule of brainstorming uses this concept. If you need an idea, you are more likely to find it in a group of many than in a group of few. Thus, in brainstorming, the more ideas the better. Somewhere in a large pile of ideas will be one or two good ones. The more ideas generated, the more effective the brainstorming session.

Beware of people carrying ideas. Beware of ideas carrying people.
—BARBARA GRIZZUTI HARRISON

Combine and Extend Ideas

While you may not criticize a particular idea, you may extend it or combine it in some way. The value of a particular idea may be the way it stimulates someone to combine or extend it. Even if your modification seems minor or obvious, say it. Don't censor yourself.

Develop the Wildest Ideas Possible

The wilder the idea, the better. It is easier to tone an idea down than to build it up. A wild idea can easily be tempered, but it is not so easy to elaborate on a simple or conservative idea.

> It does not do to leave a live dragon out of your calculations, if you live near him.
>
> —J. R. TOLKIEN

After all the ideas are generated—a period lasting no longer than 15 or 20 minutes—the entire list of ideas is evaluated, using the critical thinking skills covered throughout the textbook. The ones that are unworkable are thrown out; the ones that show promise are retained and evaluated. During this phase negative criticism is allowed.

Although brainstorming was designed as a group experience, there is some evidence to show that individual brainstorming can work even more effectively than group brainstorming (Peters 1987). As with group brainstorming, individuals brainstorming alone need to follow the same rules as the group. Be especially careful that you do not censor yourself and that you write down every idea that comes to you. Remember that these are ideas not necessarily solutions; don't be afraid to write down even the seemingly most absurd ideas.

• **Try testing brainstorming methods.** One way of doing it would be to divide up (equally and on a totally random basis) the class into two groups. One half goes into a different room and brainstorms as a group. The other half of the class brainstorms the same topic individually. Select a topic of your own or try one of these: new products for gardeners (or college students or cooks or teachers), ways of marketing panty hose to men, or advertising strategies for selling magazine subscriptions (or cologne or plants).

After a ten minute period, the brainstroming sessions are stopped. To evaluate quantity simply compare the number of different ideas generated by the brainstorming group and by the individuals. To evaluate quality, you might invite three or four or five people who did not participate in the brainstorming and who do not know what you are testing to evaluate the ideas by selecting, say, the ten or twenty best and then seeing whether the group or the individuals generated more of these ideas.

- **Try brainstorming** —either individually or in a group—with one of these topics or one of your own. Brainstorming works best when your question is one that allows for many possible answers and is phrased as an open-ended question.

  ♦ What makes for a great first date?

  ♦ What are some possible public speaking topics?

  ♦ How can we improve communication between health care workers and patients?

  ♦ What communication courses should the college add?

  ♦ What are some great opening lines (for meeting people the first time)?

  ♦ What can a speaker do to keep an audience interested?

  ♦ What are some persuasive strategies used by advertisers?

  ♦ How can we promote greater intercultural understanding?

Idea Jumping

Do you jump from idea to idea? Do you sometimes get disturbed with yourself, thinking that you are "scatter-brain" and that you don't stick with one idea long enough to develop it fully? Well, if you do, then you are

---

probably like most other people. Most thoughts last for a period shorter than a minute and over 50% of our thoughts last for 5 seconds or less! And then we jump to another thought, another idea.

Some researchers (Klinger 1990, Stine and Beranes 1994) believe that this tendency actually facilitates creative thinking because it juxtaposes a variety of ideas with the result that one idea creates associations with another idea. The result is a mixture of ideas or some new configuration of ideas.

Focus Groups

Another useful technique for creative thinking is the focus group, a kind of depth interview of a small group (Lederman 1990). The aim here is to discover what people think about an issue or product, for example, what do managers think of the new personnel policy? What do teenagers like to watch on television? Why do relationships deteriorate? What type of candy wrapping is most appealing?

In the focus group the leader tries to discover the beliefs, attitudes, thoughts, and feelings that members have so as to better guide decisions on changing the personnel policy or designing television programs or developing relationship repair strategies, or design candy wrappings? The leader's task is to prod members to analyze their thoughts and feelings on a deeper level and to use the thoughts of one member to stimulate the thoughts of others.

It is better to ask some of the questions than know all the answers.

—JAMES THURBER

CREATIVE THINKING TECHNIQUES

Let us say, for example, that you are charged with developing television programming for senior citizens, a large and affluent buying audience. You might assemble 6 to 10 senior citizens and get them talking about what they like and what they don't like about television. You might prod them with such questions as these:

- What kinds of programming do you especially like?
- What kinds of programs do you dislike?
- Do you find some programs offensive?
- What would be your ideal program?
- What types of characters do you like to see in situation comedies? In dramas?

> To think is not enough; you must think of something.
> **—JULES RENARD**

Be careful that you do not lead the focus group to respond as you might want them to. Your objective is to find out what they want, not to convince them to want what you want them to want.

- **Try the focus group.**   In small groups of five to eight, use the focus group technique to explore a question of your group's choosing or select one of these:

- What do students think about their college education?
- What do students think of contemporary music?
- What do college students think of newspapers?
- What do employees want from their employer?
- How do you feel about the current TV season?

Remember that the purpose of the focus group is not to solve a problem but just to uncover impressions, attitudes, and beliefs about the issue. In organizing your focus group, select a leader. Also develop a series of subquestions for the question you select to focus on. For example, let's say you were going to use the initial question, "What do students think about their college education?" You might want to develop subquestions to help organize the discussion, for example: What do you think of your college teachers? What do you think of the library? What do you think of the computer facilities? What do you think of the courses you took?

Organizational Uncreativity

Creative thinking theorist Arthur Van Gundy (1992) identifies a number of factors that hinder creativity in the organization. Here are just a few:

Short range focus. The motivation for quick profits may actually hinder long term innovation and growth.

Analysis preoccupation. Too much analysis may prevent new ideas from growing and developing.

Home-run mentality. Concentrating on that one big idea may result in missing the many small ideas that can make a big difference.

Managerial control emphasis. An organization is most creative when that creativity comes from all levels; if it is controlled solely by management, it will suffer from a one-sidedness.

Add-a-Tag Groups

Brainwriting

The *Add-a-Tag Group* is a form of brainwriting, the written version of brainstorming. Brainwriting uses the same four rules of brainstorming. In brainwriting members write their comments and pass them to other group members who comment on their comments (van Gundy 1987). The papers are again passed to others who write their reactions. After three or four such "passes" the papers are collected and may be discussed.

Brainwriting—and brainstorming especially—seeks creative ideas through the spontaneous interaction of group members. The Add-a-Tag group technique tries to focus on generating ideas in a more logical, systematic way. Both types of thinking are necessary, of course.

The Add-a-Tag technique will prove useful in the same situations as brainstorming. But, it will also prove especially useful as a preface to problem solving discussions where there are large differences of opinion among group members and where members may be reluctant to state their views openly. It will probably be preferred to brainstorming by those who are reluctant to voice their opinions openly as well as by those cultures who prefer this more logical and anonymous approach.

An idea isn't responsible for the people who believe in it.
—**DON MARQUIS**

Although different ways of using the add-a-tag technique will occur to you based on your own particular needs, here is one system. Each member is presented with a sheet of paper on which the particular problem is written at the top and which also contains "tags," enough for each member of the group. [A sample "Add-a-Tag" sheet is presented on page 96.] Members then write their reaction to the problem statement on one of the tags and draw a line from their tag to that part of the problem statement which their tag addresses. If the comment refers to the statement as a whole, then connect your string to the words: problem statement.

Our knowledge is the amassed thought and experience of innumerable minds.
—RALPH WALDO EMERSON

After each person has completed his or her tag, the papers are randomized and redistributed to the members who then write comments in the second tag, either as a response to the problem or as a response to the first tag. A string is drawn connecting this second tag with an elements in the problem statement or with the first tag. After all members have completed this tag, the papers are again collected, randomized, and redistributed to members who write a third tag. The process continues until the entire page is filled with comments or as long as the members feel they are adding something of value. After the final tag is written, the papers may be again collected, randomized, and redistributed to members. The Add-a-Tag papers are then read aloud to the entire group and discussed. Another alternative is to collect the papers and make them available for all members' inspection. If members feel—after they have inspected the papers—that another meeting or discussion is necessary, it will be called.

The group may decide on a number of variations for writing tags. For example, the group might prescribe that only positive comments (or only negative comments) can be made. Or the instructions may be extremely general, for example, "elaborate on anything you wish." Another technique is to label each tag with the type of comment you want the group to address itself to.

Thus, for example, the first tag may be labeled "cost." When members write their first tag it must in some way relate to cost factors. Another tag might be labeled "getting more information." Members would here have to indicate whether they felt they could secure more information on the problem.

- **Try using the Add-a-Tag group technique.** In a group of five or six, select a topic that is of interest to your group members (or use one suggested below) and prepare an Add-a-Tag form for each member. Seated in a circle each member begins to respond to the problem statement on the first tag and repeat the process until all tags are used or until members feel they are no longer coming up with any good ideas. Some suitable topics might be:

♦ How can we improve the physical health of our employees?

♦ How can we become more effective parents?

♦ How can we increase the sales of reference books such as the dictionary and the thesaurus?

♦ How can we make this campus more culturally aware and sensitive?

♦ How can we maintain a cleaner city?

♦ How can we reduce sexism? racism? homophobia?

♦ How can we save time and work more efficiently?

♦ How can we be more socially responsible?

♦ How can we publicize AIDS Awareness Day?

♦ How can we help save the earth?

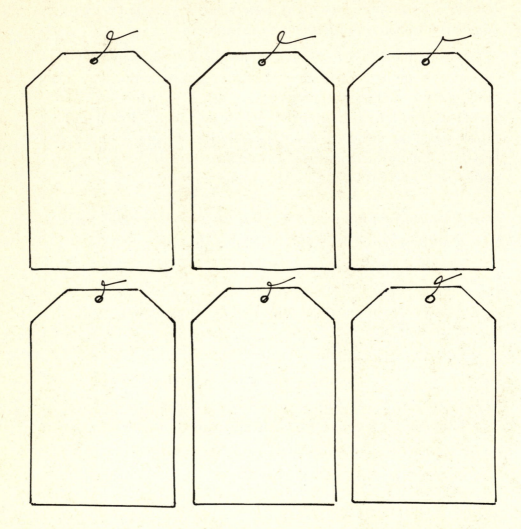

Another Puzzling Assumption

```
         o              o  o  o  o
       o   o              o  o  o
     o   o   o             o   o
   o   o   o   o              o
        (A)                  (B)
```

Try to change Figure A into Figure B by moving only 3 circles. Try this for a few minutes before reading on.

If you have difficulty with this, it is likely that you are focusing your attention on moving the top 3 circles. The unstated assumptions might be:

1. the rows with fewest circles should be moved
2. entire rows must be moved

These are assumptions that many people make and that prevent solving the problem. The solution is illustrated on page 106.

Logographic Analysis

I call this technique "logographic" and the form used a "logogram" from the Greek *logo* meaning *word* and the *gram* or *graph* in the sense of map or mapping. Thus, a logogram is a map of words that describes the territory (problem, question, organizational area, etc.). Logographic analysis is a technique for generating ideas quickly either alone or in a group situation from a pre-existing set of terms. This list of terms—ideas actually— form the basis for the analysis of a specific question or problem.

Whether a thought is a dud depends also on the head it hits.
—STANISLAW J. LEC

> Eliminate all other factors, and the one which remains must be the truth.
>
> **—SHERLOCK HOLMES**

The terms in the logogram are specifically chosen to shed some light on the topic at hand. So, there would be different logograms for different types of problems. The effectiveness of the logographic analysis, then, depends greatly on the effectiveness of the words in the logogram. If the words are poorly chosen, then the analysis is likely to suffer.

The Feelings Logogram, presented below on page 101, is designed to illustrate a logogram for exploring feeling states and might be used, for example, by a group to explore their emotional reactions to specific happenings or people, or by a couple to explore their feelings after a traumatic event. Note that the terms are presented in alphabetical order so that each item is treated independently rather than as part of a semantically related cluster. The Cost/Benefits Logogram, presented below on page 102, is designed to illustrate a logogram that might be used in evaluating the new fringe benefits package or the proposed merger of various departments or two competing health plans. Both logograms are illustrative; original logograms should be constructed for each unique situation. A place to write your focus is provided for both of these. This may prove useful when you want each group member to focus on the same specific issue.

Logograms similar to those presented here are distributed to the group members who are instructed to circle, say, the three terms (or ten terms or twenty terms) that best explain how they feel about the particular problem.

You can focus the responses on any particular issue you wish. For example, an advertising team working on a television ad for a new product might want to focus on—at one stage—the desired images that they want the product to suggest. So, they might create a logogram of a few hundred potential images. A group concerned with worker morale might develop a logogram centering on those factors that influence morale, for example, communication patterns, working environment, management attitudes, and so on.

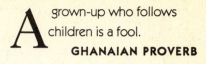

A grown-up who follows children is a fool.
GHANAIAN PROVERB

Age and Creativity

Two widely different views of creativity are held by theorists. On the one hand is the theory that children are extremely creative and that our conditioning gradually destroys this natural urge. On the other hand, there is the view that knowledge of and work within a field of study are necessary for generating creative ideas (Dormen and Edidin 1989, Stine and Benares 1994). In surveys of creativity, for example, it is found that many of the great works were produced when the person had spent approximately 10 years at the general task. For instance, Einstein began work on relativity at around 16 but didn't make his big discovery until some 10 years later. Mozart produced his best works at around 22; he had been writing music, however, for at least 10 years prior to this.

The child-like characteristics of innocence, being unafraid of failure, and being willing to try anything, coupled with in-depth knowledge of the subject and usually long work in the field, combine to produce creative ideas— ideas that are new and useful. The child, it seems, just produces what's new; the average person (adult) produces what's useful. It is the creative person (most often an adult with significant work experience in the field) who produces what is both new and useful.

Perhaps the greatest advantage of logographic analysis is that it is easy to set up for any specific task, for example:

♦ As an ice-breaker for getting group members to interact and learn something about each other, each member might be provided with a simple logogram of, say, sociological characteristics. Each member would then select, say, five characteristics that apply to her or him and discuss these.

♦ As a conflict resolution tool, the logogram might contain the 100 or 200 of the most commonly identified issues that cause problems in interpersonal relationships. Each person might then review the logogram and begin to talk about, say, the three most important concepts on the page.

♦ As a research tool, it might be used to focus the subjects in a study on a specific field of meaning and ask them to select, say, the three most important characteristics of a potential lifetime partner, or the four most annoying habits of the opposite sex, or the five most credible professions, and so on.

• **Try using logographic analysis** in a group of five or six. Use the accompanying Feelings Logogram to discuss your feelings about college life, prospects for the future, your relationship lives, or any topic that allows members to share their feelings. Or use the accompanying Cost/Benefits Logogram to discuss your reactions to a particular proposal, decision, proposed solution to a problem, or policy. This will give you some experience with using a logogram to stimulate ideas and will enable you to better understand the characteristics of an effective logogram.

A Feelings Logogram

Feeling Focus:_____.

absorbing	complimented	engrossed	irritated	sad
acrimonious	concerned	enjoying	jolted	satisfied
active	concerned	enraged	joyful	scared
affirming	confident	enraptured	loathful	scorned
against	confirmed	equal	lonely	secondary
aggressive	conflicted	esteemed	loud	secure
amazed	contemptful	exasperated	loving	shocked
amazed	contented	excluded	melancholy	sick
angry	curious	expressive	mindful	sleepy
annoyed	current	fascinated	mindless	snubbed
anxious	dated	fearful	miserable	soft
anxious	dejected	flexible	nauseous	sorry
appealing	delighted	formal	negative	spicy
apprehensive	depressed	forsaken	noticed	startled
argumentative	determined	friendly	offended	strong
assertive	disconfirmed	frightened	open-eyed	sturdy
astonished	discriminated	functional	outraged	submissive
attending	disdainful	furious	passive	supported
attentive	disgusted	glad	phobic	surprised
avoidant	disgustful	grateful	pleased	terrorized
aware	dismal	grieving	pleased	trepidating
awed	dispensable	happy	positive	troubled
bashful	displeased	harassed	powerful	unaware
believable	disrespected	helpless	powerless	uncertain
belligerent	distant	hopeful	practical	unhappy
bitter	distasteful	hostile	primary	unhappy
blameful	distressed	impressed	reconciled	vigorous
blissful	disturbed	included	rejected	weak
busy	dogmatic	incredulous	repugnant	well-adjusted
bypassed	doubtful	indignant	repulsed	wondering
caught-off-	dreading	ineffective	resentful	worrying
guard	dynamic	informal	resistful	zestful
certain	ecstatic	insecure	reticent	_____
cheerful	effective	insolent	revulsed	_____
cheerful	empathic	insulted	ridiculed	_____
close	enchanted	interested	rigid	_____
complacent	engaged	involved	romantic	_____

Figure 5. A Cost/Benefits Logogram.

Cost/Benefits Focus:_____.

accountability	damage	fortunate	nullify	satisfactory
advantageous	damages	frustrate	odds	satisfying
advantages	damaging	fulfilling	operative	seasonable
affirmative	dated	functional	opportune	selfish
anachronistic	dear	futuristic	optimistic	selfless
annihilate	demolish	gain	overdone	senseless
anxiety provok-	denounce	gratifying	pay	sensible
ing	deny	gross	pleasing	serviceable
apathetic	destroy	handicap	positive	set back
approve	destructive	harmful	practical	spoil
assenting	detrimental	heterogeneous	privilege	static
auspicious	disadvantageous	homogeneous	productive	timely
bargain	disapprove	hopeful	profit	trendy
blemish	disavow	idealistic	profits	underdone
beneficial	discomfort	impractical	propitious	unproductive
benefits	discount	income	quench	unsatisfactory
blessing	disfigure	indulgent	questionable	useful
boon	dynamic	ineffective	quixotic	useless
botch	earnings	ineffectual	realistic	Utopian
bottom line	edge	injurious	receipts	veto
cheap	efficiency	logical	reject	wages
compensation	emotional	lose	remuneration	win
competent	empathic	loss	repudiate	work hours
concurring	empowering	lucky	returns	working
confirming	excessive	mar	revenue	worthless
constructive	exorbitant	megatrend	romantic	_____
contradict	expenses	morale	ruin	_____
convenient	expensive	necessary	salary	_____
costly	extravagant	negative	sanction	_____
costs	faddish	net	satiate	_____

CREATIVE THINKING TECHNIQUES

Once you have used a logogram, you are ready to construct one of your own. Either individually or in a small group, construct a logogram for a specific purpose. Here are a few titles to get you started. Use one of these or one of your own: a gender exploration logogram (to help discuss sexual harassment and sexual discrimination), a perceptual logogram (to share perspectives or points of view), a learning logogram (to assess cognitive and emotional learning), a problem-solving logogram (to resolve the mailroom bottleneck), a cultural awareness logogram (to promote intercultural understanding), a relationship logogram (to resolve interpersonal conflicts or to enrich a relationship).

If doing this in a group situation, you might then work with each of the logograms and actually try to accomplish one of the aims for which the logogram was originally constructed. Does the logographic analysis give you any useful insights? Does it facilitate discussion?

Self-Assessment 2:
How Creative Do You See Yourself Now?

Now that you've read through this booklet, reassess your perception of yourself as a creative thinker. Don't look at how you answered this self-assessment form earlier (at least not until you have competed this one). After you have completed this form, compare it with the form you completed before beginning this study of creativity. You should find not only a greater understanding of creative thinking and how it operates but also an increase in your own creativity.

1. On the basis of your past performance, how creative do you see yourself?

   _____ very creative

   _____ fairly creative

   _____ in the middle

   _____ fairly uncreative

   _____ very uncreative

2. How often do you get creative ideas?

   _____ at least once a day

   _____ a few a week

   _____ a few a month

   _____ one a month

   _____ less than one a month

3. In what areas are you most creative? For example, in what academic areas are you most creative? Least creative? How do you account for the differences?

4. In what aspects of your personal, social, and professional life does creativity now play a role?

5. What role will creative thinking have in your life ten years from now?

6. Have you ever had what you would consider a peak creative experience? Describe it.

7. What was your last creative idea? What did you do with it?

Answers/Solutions:

For exercise on Page 54

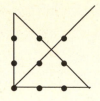

The solution requires that you go beyond the "square." The solution is extremely simple but not if you define the problem as one involving a square.

For exercise on Page 59
Here are the remote associates for the triads. There may be other remote associates that are equally or even more appropriate than those given here.

1. soda	7. blue	13. spider	20. door	27. ball
2. yellow	8. white	14. chair	21. hall	28. house
3. table	9. glass	15. school	22. shirt	29. book
4. love	10. red	16. table	23. pen	30. picture
5. televi-sion	11. medical	17. card	24. potato	
6. box	12. insur-ance	18. room	25. book	
		19. storm	26. bridge	

For exercise on Page 97
Because only three circles can be moved, many people don't even think of moving the circles in the row of four.

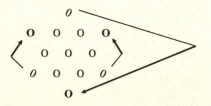

POSTSCRIPT
Communicating New Ideas

After generating and developing your ideas, either individually or as a member of a team, it will often be necessary to communicate them to others. If you are a manager of a company, it may involve your implementing the new ideas, hopefully with a receptive audience. Your textbook covers the principles and skills you'll need in getting new ideas understood, accepted, and implemented. Here, it's only necessary to highlight briefly some guidelines that are especially appropriate to introducing new ideas. These guidelines are designed to get you thinking about how to present a new idea to an organization, a relationship partner, or a family. Although these general guidelines will prove useful in most situations, there will be situations in which they would not be appropriate. Consider these, then, as possible options for some situations in which you want to communicate new ideas.

> We can communicate an idea around the world in seventy seconds, but it sometimes takes years for an idea to get through 1/4" of human skull.
> **—CHARLES F. KETTERING**

- Attach the new idea to an old one if possible. People are more apt to understand and accept new ideas when they somehow resemble old and more comfortable ones. If it's a new rule, show how it's related to the old rule.

- Present the idea in a nonthreatening manner. New ideas often frighten people. If your ideas might lead people to feel insecure about their jobs, then alleviate these worries before you try to explain the idea in any detail. And, generally, it is best to proceed slowly.

An idea, like a ghost (according to the common notion of a ghost), must be spoken to a little before it will explain itself.

—CHARLES DICKENS

♦ Present new ideas tentatively. You may be taken with the flash of inspiration, but have not worked out the practical implications of the idea. So, if you present your ideas tentatively and they are shown to be impractical or unworkable, you will be less hurt psychologically and—most important—will be more willing to try presenting new ideas again.

♦ In many instances, it will prove helpful to link changes and new ideas to perceived problems in the organization or relationship. If you are going to ask employees to complete extensive surveys, then show them how this extra work will correct a problem and benefit them and the organization.

♦ Say why you think the idea would work. Give the advantages of your plan over the existing situation and explain why you think this idea should be implemented. The patterns for organizing a public speech will prove helpful in accomplishing this.

♦ State the negatives (usually there are some with most ideas) as you understand them and, of course, why you think the positives outweigh them.

♦ Relate the new ideas to the needs and interests of those on whom the innovation will impact.

♦ Persuasion research would suggest that you proceed inductively when you anticipate objections. When presenting ideas to a hostile or potentially hostile audience, give the benefits before introducing the new idea. Ideally, you'd move your audience into wanting the benefits and values of the new idea before they ever hear of the idea itself.

In responding to new ideas, be careful of tendencies toward groupthink, the tendency to be swayed by what the other members of the group or organization think. Appropriate responses to creativity will often run counter to the majority opinion, if only because there seems a natural tendency to resist change. Focus first on the idea, make sure you understand it and its implications. Then, consider what others are saying.

A particularly good technique to use in responding to new ideas is PIP'N. Like so many creative thinking tools, this one comes from combining the insights from other techniques. In this case, the paraphrase notion comes from Carl Rogers and the interesting, positive, and negative aspects come from Edward de-Bono's PMI (Plus or positive, minus or negative, and interesting). Combined and reorganized, we get PIP'N. It involves four steps:

> It takes two to speak the truth—one to speak and another to hear.
> **—HENRY DAVID THOREAU**

P = **Paraphrase.** State in your own words what you think the other person is saying. This will ensure that you and the person proposing the idea are talking about the same thing. Your paraphrase will also provide the other person with the opportunity to elaborate or clarify his or her ideas.

> It seemed rather incongruous that in a society of supersophisticated communication, we often suffer from a shortage of listeners.
> **—ERMA BOMBECK**

I = **Interesting.** State something interesting that you find in the idea. Say why you think this idea might be interesting to you, to others, to the organization.

P = **Positive.** Say something positive about the idea. What is good about it? How might it solve a problem or make a situation better?

N = **Negative.** State any negatives that you think the idea might entail. Might it prove expensive? Difficult to implement? Is it directed at insignificant issues?

Having completed **Brainstorms** (and together with your communication course, textbook and especially your own experiences), you should now be a more creative and critical thinker. You should also have considerable understanding of communication and a mastery of important communication skills. Combined, they will serve you well. Have fun.

I train myself for triumph by knowing it is mine no matter what.

—AUDRE LORDE

Sources and Suggested Readings

Here is a master list of both the sources cited in the text and readings that would make useful additions to what you read here. Recommended readings are prefaced by an asterisk and are annotated. Try to add a few of these books (most are in paperback) to your personal library. Regardless of your specific interpersonal, social, or professional experiences, you will always find creative thinking useful.

It is chiefly through books that we enjoy intercourse with superior minds.

—**WILLIAM ELLERY CHANNING**

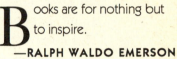

ooks are for nothing but to inspire.

—**RALPH WALDO EMERSON**

*Adams, James L. (1986). *Conceptual Block-busting: A Guide to Better Ideas*, 3rd ed. Reading, MA: Addison-Wesley.
   This excellent book covers the various blocks to learning that many people have, such as perceptual, emotional, cultural, intellectual, and expressive. Special attention is given to groups and organizations.

Albarn, Keith and Jenny Miall Smith (1977). *Diagram: The Instrument of Thought.* London: Thames and Hudson.

Albrecht, Karl (1980). *Brain Power: Learn to Improve Your Thinking Skills.* Englewood Cliffs, NY: Prentice-Hall.

Asimov, Isaac (1983). Write, Write, Write. *Communicator's Journal* (May/June).

Berko, Jean (1958). The Child's Learning of English Morphology. *Word* 14:150-177.

*deBono, Edward (1968). *New Think: The Use of Lateral Thinking in the Generation of New Ideas.* New York: Avon.
   This book sets forth deBono's concept of lateral thinking, thinking that is not logical or linear but that attacks problems

from different perspectives. deBono has written many other useful books on creative and critical thinking; your bookstore is likely to have several of them.

deBono, Edward (1969). *The Mechanism of Mind*. New York: Simon and Schuster.

deBono, Edward (1976). *Teaching Thinking*. New York: Penguin.

deBono, Edward (1978). *Opportunities: A Handbook of Business Opportunity Search*. New York: Penguin.

*deBono, Edward (1991). *Six Action Shoes*. New York: HarperBusiness.
On the analogy of the six thinking hats, deBono here presents six shoes, six types of action and ranges from routines and formal procedure, explosions and danger, warmth and domesticity, sensible and practical, inevitable, and imperial authority. For each type of action, deBono offers unusual insight into the thinking that goes into each of these types of actions.

*DePorter, Bobbi with Mike Hernacki (1992). *Quantum Learning: Unleashing the Genius in You*. New York: Dell.
A general work on all aspects of learning and how to increase the efficiency of your learning. Covers creative thinking as well as critical thinking, memory, writing with confidence, note taking, and how to discover your own personal learning style.

Dormen, Lesley and Peter Edidin (1989). Original Spin. *Psychology Today* (July/August).

Gazzaniga, Michael S. (1988). *Mind Matters: How Mind and Brain Interact to Create Our Conscious Lives*. Boston, MA: Houghton Mifflin.

Gevins, Alan, et al. (1981). Electrical Potentials in the Human Brain During Cognition. *Science* 213 (August 21): 918-922.

Goleman, Daniel (1992). Your Unconscious Mind May be Smarter Than You. *New York Times* (June 23), Section C, p. 1.

Gordon, William J. J. (1961). *Synectics: The Development of Creative Capacity*. New York: Harper & Row.

*Gross, Ronald (1991). *Peak Learning: A Master Course in Learning How to Learn*. Los Angeles: Jeremy P. Tarcher, Inc.
A general work devoted to improving your learning abilities and covers such topics as building your confidence as a learner, discovering your unique learning style, improving your memory and reading skills, and developing both critical and creative thinking abilities.

Guilford, J. P. (1975). Creativity: A Quarter Century of Progress. In I. A. Taylor and J. W. Getzels, eds. *Perspectives in Creativity*. Chicago: Aldine Publishing Co.

Hanks, Kurt, Larry Belliston, and Dave Edwards (1978). *Design Yourself*. Los Altos, CA: William Kaufmann, Inc.

Harrison, Allen F. and Robert M. Bramson (1984). *The Art of Thinking*. New York: Berkely.

*Higgins, James M. *101 Creative Problem Solving Techniques*. New York: New Management Publishing Co., 1994.
Contains a wide variety of creative thinking techniques with step by step procedures for many of them.

*Ideafisher (1994). IdeaFisher Systems, Inc.
This is a powerful computer program that enables you to generate ideas based on prepared questions and lists of terms. If you have a computer and want to generate lots of ideas for a wide variety of topics, get this program.

*Johnson, Kenneth G., ed. (1991). *Thinking Creatically*. Englewood, NJ: Institute of General Semantics.
Offers 23 articles on the general semantics perspective on
thinking and especially on combining critical and creative
thinking (hence the title of the book). Also offers a forward
by Steve Allen and an annotated list of books.

Klinger, Eric (1990). *Daydreaming*. Los Angeles, CA: Jeremy P.
Tarcher.

Koberg, Don and Jim Bagnall (1976a). *The Universal Traveler*. Los
Altos, CA: William Kaufmann, Inc.

Koberg, Don and Jim Bagnall (1976b). *Values Tech: A Portable School
for Discovering and Developing Decision-Making Skills for Self-En-
hancing Potentials*. Los Altos, CA: William Kaufmann, Inc.

*Kohl, Herbert (1992). *From Archetype to Zeitgeist: Powerful Ideas for
Powerful Thinking*. Boston, MA: Little, Brown and Company.
A wonderful guide through the important concepts from literature, the arts, psychology, economics, political science,
critical thinking, logic and reasoning, anthropology and lin-
guistics, religion, and more.

Lanagan, Leonara M. and Susan M. Watkins (1987). Human Factors. *Psychology Today* (October).

Langer, Ellen (1987). *Mindfulness*. Reading, MA: Addison-Wesley.

Marks, Lawrence E. (1975). Synesthesia: The Lucky People with
Mixed-up Senses. *Psychology Today* 9 (June):48-52.

*McCarthy, Michael J. (1991). *Mastering the Information Age: A
Course in Working Smarter, Thinking Better, and Learning Faster*.
Los Angeles: Jeremy P. Tarcher.
Covers a variety of thinking aids such as developing your
memory, reading actively and faster, thinking critically, over-

coming research anxiety, and communicating information more effectively.

*McCartland, Grace (1994). *Thunderbolt Thinking*. Austin, TX: Bernard-Davis.
This book is built around 25 techniques to improve your thinking, especially on the job.

Mednick, Sarnoff A. (1962). The Associative Basis of the Creative Process. *Psychological Review* 69:220-232.

*Michalko, Michael (1991). *Tinkertoys: A Handbook of Business Creativity for the 90's*. Berkeley, CA: Ten Speed Press.
Offers a collection of creative thinking techniques with lots of practical examples from the world of business.

*Miller, William C. (1987). *The Creative Edge: Fostering Innovation Where You Work*. Reading, MA: Addison-Wesley.
A comprehension guide to creativity at work; covers such areas as developing yourself as a creative thinker, linear techniques, intuitive techniques, how to deal with blocks to creativity, and how to work with creative groups.

*Olson, Robert T. (1980). *The Art of Creative Thinking*. New York: Harper & Row.
Covers the obstacles to creative thinking, creativity in problem solving, and numerous creative thinking techniques. Also explains how to transform your ideas into action.

Peters, Roger (1987). *Practical Intelligence: Working Smarter in Business and the Professions*. New York: HarperCollins.

*Raudsepp, Eugene (1981). *How Creative Are You?* New York: Perigee Books.
Covers blocks and barriers to creativity and characteristics of the creative individual. An extensive self-test of your creative thinking style and ability is also included.

*Raudsepp, Eugene (1987). *Growth Games for the Creative Manager.*
New York: Perigee Books.
Offers 50 games that a manager can use to expand creative
management practices, skills, and abilities.

Rice, Berkeley (1984). Imagination to Go. *Psychology Today* 18
(May):48-56.

Richards, Ruth L., Dennis K. Kinney, Maria Benet, and Ann Mer-
zel (1988). Everyday Creativity: Characteristics of the Lifetime
Creativity Scales and Validation with Three Large Samples.
Journal of Personality and Social Psychology 54:476-485.

Rossi, Ernest (1989). *The 20-minute Break: The New Science of Ultra-
dian Rhythms.* Los Angeles, CA: Jeremy P. Tarcher.

Ruggiero, Vincent Ryan (1991). *The Art of Thinking: A Guide to Critical and Creative Thought,* 3rd ed. New York: HarperCollins.

Simonton, Dean K. (1990). Creativity and Wisdom in Aging. In
Handbook of the Psychology of Aging, ed. James Birren and
Warner Schaie. New York: Academic Press, pp. 320-329.

*Stine, Jean and Camden Benares (1994). *It's All in Your Head: Re-
markable Facts about the Human Mind.* New York: Prentice
Hall General Reference.
This book contains a wealth of tidbits about thinking and the
brain. Many of the boxes presented here were suggested by
Stine and Benares.

Thayer, Robert E. (1988). Energy Walks. *Psychology Today* (October).

*Thompson, Charles "Chic" (1992). *What a Great Idea! The Key
Steps Creative People Take.* New York: HarperPerennial.
An excellent general work on creativity organized into four
parts: freedom (the nature of creativity), expression (explor-

ing and understanding the problem), creation (the idea generating process itself), and action (evaluating and managing new ideas).

VanGundy, Arthur B. (1987). *Creative Problem Solving*. New York: Quorum Books.

*VanGundy, Arthur B. (1992). *Idea Power: Techniques & Resources to Unleash the Creativity in Your Organization*. New York: Amacom [American Management Association].
A great guide to creative thinking for just about any business or organization; much, however, is applicable to creative thinking in any area.

*VanGundy, Arthur B. (1995). *Brain Boosters for Business Advantage*. San Diego, CA: Pfeiffer and Company.
Another excellent work on creative thinking applied to business with 101 brain boosters and a useful guide to the expanding area of software programs designed to help you be more creative.

Vernon, Philip E. (1986). *The Dictionary of Developmental and Educational Psychology*, ed. Rom Harre and Roger Lamb. Cambridge, Mass.: MIT Press.

*von Oech, Roger (1990). *A Whack on the Side of the Head: How You Can Be More Creative*, rev. ed. New York: Warner Books.
One of the best books on practical suggestions for increasing your creative thinking. von Oech followed this popular book with *A Kick in the Seat of the Pants: Using Your Explorer, Artist, Judge, & Warrior to be More Creative*. New York: Warner Books, 1993.

*von Savant, Marilyn and Laniary Fleischer (1991). *Brain Building in Just 12 Weeks*. New York: Bantam Books.

A 12-week course in improving your abilities to think and learn, and covers such topics as vocabulary building, communication skills, developing your intuitive sense, and improving your reading.

Wade, Carol and Carol Tavris (1993). *Psychology*, 3rd ed. New York: HarperCollins.

White, Kristin. (1993). How the Mind Ages. *Psychology Today* 26 (November/December):38-42, 79-80, 91-95.

*Wujec, Tom (1988). *Pumping Ions: Games and Exercises to Flex Your Mind.* New York: Doubleday.
Offers a wealth of insights into creative thinking and provides lots of exercises to practice the skills.

Zwicky, Fritz (1957). *Morphological Analysis*. Berlin: Springer.

Instructor Reaction Form for
BRAINSTORMS

Please complete this form and return it to:

Communications Editor
HarperCollins College Publishers
10 East 53rd Street
New York, New York 10022

1. Describe your course and class, for example, course title and level, the course goals, the nature of the student body.

2. Did you use **Brainstorms** in your class? If so, in what way? If not, what were your reasons?

3. What did you like best about **Brainstorms**?

4. What did you like least about **Brainstorms**?

5. What changes would you like to see in future editions, including, for example, new topics, expansion, reduction, or deletion of topics included here?

6. Any additional comments or sugggestions you'd care to share would be much appreciated.

If you wish, send any comments to author via e-mail
(JDEVITO@SHIVA.HUNTER.CUNY.EDU)

Student Reaction Form for
BRAINSTORMS

Please complete this form and return it to:

Communications Editor
HarperCollins College Publishers
10 East 53rd Street
New York, New York 10022

1. In what course are you enrolled? Please give title of course and school.

2. What percentage of **Brainstorms** did you read?

3. What did you like best about **Brainstorms**?

4. What did you like least about **Brainstorms**?

5. Compared with other textbooks and course readings, how would you
   rate **Brainstorms**?
   ___ much more relevant and useful
   ___ more relevant and useful
   ___ about the same
   ___ less relevant and useful
   ___ much less relevant and useful

6. How could **Brainstorms** be made more useful to you?

7. Any additional comments or suggestions you'd care to share would be
   greatly appreciated.

If you wish, send any comments to author via e-mail
(JDEVITO@SHIVA.HUNTER.CUNY.EDU)